Lies of Mercy
Lies of Grace

Tales of a Pennsylvania Dutch
Girl in MIAMI

Carol Jo Pettit

With Love,

To Glenn and Sharyn,
who lived the story with me,

To Don,
whose love and support sustained me,

And to Steve and Ginger,
who always believed in me.

Also by Carol Jo Pettit

Second Diagnosis

Chapter 1

"The last temptation is the greatest treason.
To do the right deed for the wrong reason."
T.S. Eliot

Right and Wrong. I've thought about that a lot, my father having instructed me in the difference between the two. Telling the truth is Right. Telling a lie is Wrong. Simple to understand. Difficult to execute. I'll tell you the truth as I remember it. That seems Right to me.

My growing up years in Miami were a lot like the Key West lime pie we loved—first you encounter the smooth, dulcet flavor. Then you detect the tang beneath. No one could have grown up in the South in the 1940s and 50s without having experienced some bitter in the sweet.

My name is Mercedes Grace Malone, but everyone calls me Mercy. I'm half Irish and half Pennsylvania Dutch, which, of course, is really just German. Those two lifestyles created a zig-zag when we children were growing up. Always a swing between Mother's no-nonsense Pennsylvania Dutch outlook and Dad's Irish view that not much was worthy of being taken too seriously. We three kids held on tightly and swung with the zig and the zag of our lives. I probably should tell you that the zig of the Pennsylvania Dutch was stronger than the zag of the Irish.

My mother's folks on her father's side were Amish a few generations back, and were part of the German society that settled in Pennsylvania and Ohio in the 1700s and 1800s.

1

Up North, our little Miami family would have fit in perfectly, but the remnants of the Pennsylvania Dutch language and the remnants of a very conservative culture emerged regularly and made us stand out Down South.

Like Mardi Gras. While most of the South was celebrating with costumes and parties and spiked punch and other delicious forms of sin we'd heard about, our family was sitting at home dunking *fasnachts* (doughnuts) into steaming cups of cocoa to honor Fasnacht Day, the night before the beginning of Lent. Now think about it. If you were fourteen, would you rather be dressed up like an Arabian princess in a bewitching blue satin costume and a sequined veil which only let your eyes show, dancing with a boy in a pirate's costume and mask, hoping he was the cute basketball player two rows over in your algebra class, or would you rather be curled up on the couch in your living room in last year's faded pink chenille bathrobe, dunking doughnuts with a very prim someone who told you to "eat yourself up of *fasnachts*"? That's the way we were different. That's the way we were conspicuous.

When we were young, my brother Joe and I didn't know we sometimes stood out. We just ran like crazy every summer morning with the neighborhood kids and hid from the sun every summer afternoon, sitting cross-legged and leaning our steaming backs against the merciful cool cement of the east side of the house. There we gulped down huge, sweating pitchers of frigid cherry Kool-Aid and cracked the remnants of melting ice cubes with our teeth. We talked about virtually everything, well, everything that wouldn't bring on a reprimand from our parents, like where our new baby came from or who Santa Claus really was. I learned a lot during those afternoon conferences, although it was sometimes hard to accept life's facts and truths from people with sticky, red Kool-Aid moustaches. Imagine a skinny, bare-footed boy with no shirt expounding on what the

2

sound barrier was all about while sporting lips that looked like the red wax ones you could buy at Holly's Five and Dime for two cents.

It was during such an afternoon session that our neighbor Mikey LeRoy Smithson told me my initials stood for a movie studio in Hollywood, California. Then he told Claude Pickens and me that our names had other meanings. Understandably, Claude wasn't much interested, but I felt as important as that stuck up Sally Sue Van Landingham in my third grade class. Needing to know immediately what Mikey LeRoy had in mind, I ran from the group and slammed through the front door, making the ornamental aluminum flamingo flap his wings against the screen like a goose on the attack. Once inside, I dragged the huge dictionary out of the bookcase and down to the floor, and flipped to the M's.

Menu, meow. Hey, I know these words. *Mephitic, mercantile.* Yikes! *Mercurous, mercury, Mercury, mercy.* There I am, *mer-cy* kind or compassionate.

I didn't understand what compassionate meant, but I did know something about being kind. My father had already included that in his list of Rights and Wrongs. It is not kind to say something mean about someone. That is Wrong. It is kind to make someone feel good. That is Right.

Feeling pretty confident about mercy, I turned back to the G's and sought *grace.* There it is—*grace* beauty of motion, to dignify or honor, having a sense of what is decent. That needed some explanation. After a quick conference with my mother, I had a fuzzy picture of someone with grace and mercy, and it was overwhelming. Mother told me not to worry—it just meant some people knew what was Right, and they acted that way. Simple to understand. Difficult to execute.

The Irish flattery I felt with my names soon turned into a Pennsylvania Dutch burden, and they quickly became THE

NAMES and dominated my life. How could I possibly live up to THE NAMES? No one asked me to, but I thought I needed to behave like someone who had been given important names and knew what to do with them. Besides, with the frizzy Toni Home Permanent Wave Mother had inflicted on me and made that stuck up Sally Sue Van Landingham say my head looked like a dead chrysanthemum, I didn't feel very pretty. With THE NAMES, I felt as beautiful as Doris Day, but, of course, without the freckles.

It was easy for me to forget the responsibility of THE NAMES most of the time, but the idea remained in my brain and gave me something besides Dickie Barnes in Mrs. Martin's third grade class to daydream about. Because of THE NAMES, I found myself going on watch for infractions of Right and Wrong, like a room monitor trying to impress the teacher, and when I noticed the infractions, I was reminded that there were nicer ways of doing or saying things. Like when Mikey LeRoy told Joe he was too smart, and one of the guys at school didn't like him because he made him look bad in class. I knew it was Right to tell the truth, but saw the truth could hurt, and that felt Wrong. So I decided to question people in authority.

I spotted my first expert when Otis-the-Egg-Man drove out of the mansions' back dirt driveway and into our front driveway.

"Otis-the-Egg-Man, do you always have to tell the truth, even when it may hurt someone's feelings?" I asked.

"Y'all should tell the truth all the time, Miss Mercy, no exceptions," Otis explained as he tucked a few reddish-brown chicken feathers into the egg carton, making a most pleasant arrangement, bird nest style . . . no extra charge.

"The results don't matter," Otis continued. "A man's integrity is the most important thing to him." Startled by his own oratorical skills, Otis bolted upright, pushed his crushed

4

wool hat back farther on his damp, shiny head, and dropped the dime into his leather change purse, which was as crackled and dark as his old-man's face.

I stared at the egg nest and listened as Otis offered several examples. He said sometimes he had to be frank with folks—but, of course, not white folks—and I realized Otis' way would be doing the Right thing for the Wrong reason. Simple to understand. Simple to execute. I went for a dainty exit, and with the carton cradled in my arm like Mother held the baby, I leaped off the running board of his rickety old truck, license plate number Dade County OU812. Joe said the number was some sort of secret code. Otis climbed back into the front seat and drove off looking proud and honest.

After supper that night I approached Billy Wayne Perkins, the curly haired teenager my parents sometimes hired because Joe felt he was too old to have a babysitter. Billy was like having an older friend visit. It helped Joe's pride a little.

"Billy Wayne, should you always tell the truth, even if it may hurt someone's feelings?" I asked. Billy Wayne looked at me like I was from Mars. He rubbed his dirty hands down the front of his dirty dungarees and said that stuff didn't matter and just get the Coke out of the fridge while he got the rum. I was beginning to wonder about the validity of my experts. I'd have to be more selective.

The next morning I awoke to a sweet fragrance and followed it into our kitchen. There was Mother using the bottom of her pansy flowered apron as a pot holder to pull the kettle of bubbling apple *busser* (butter) off the stove. She wiped the clammy dampness from her forehead with the back of her tiny wrist and pushed a black curl off her face.

"Dip out a spoonful for your toast of busser," she suggested in her best Pennsylvania Dutch way. "And eat yourself done." She must be tired already, I thought. Mother only spoke that way when she was tired or excited, unless, of course, it just slipped out.

Blowing on the apple butter, and nibbling the sweet cream on my toast, I asked my question, "Momma, is it better to always tell the truth, even when it will hurt someone's feelings?"

Mother put the big kettle spoon down on the cracked saucer she used as a drip plate, smoothed the wrinkles out of her apron, and turned her full attention to me and my question.

"You'll have to make that decision yourself, Mercy," she told me very slowly and very thoughtfully. "Most of the time, only the truth matters, but sometimes it's more important to spare someone, to offer hope or support."

It was then that it all made sense.

It was then that I understood about lies of mercy. And lies of grace.

They are scattered throughout my life.

Chapter 2

"And in that town a dog was found.
As many dogs there be,
Both mongrel, puppy, whelp, and hound,
And curs of low degree."
- Oliver Goldschmidt

"You want me to take yer dog where to do what?" the man on the other end of the line yelled so loudly that everyone in Mrs. P.K. Tucker's crowded little living room could hear quite clearly. At the time, Mrs. P.K. Tucker had the only phone on the block, and she enjoyed the notoriety and the company the heavy black instrument afforded her.

"Don't make me say it, please, again," my mother appealed to the voice.

Some kind person somewhere in my mother's life had let her choose any pup she wanted from his dog Big Sugar's litter of pure-bred mongrels. Mother enjoyed scratching and petting and cooing with Big Sugar so much that she decided she had to have the pup that most resembled her. Big Sugar, that is, not Mother. And just to carry on the tradition and to better ensure the same pleasing personality as the bitch's—Big Sugar's, that is—the puppy was named Baby Sugar.

Mother spoiled Baby Sugar the way a Pennsylvania Dutch woman couldn't chance spoiling her own children. Joe and I were much too valuable to be allowed third helpings

7

of *smearcase* (cottage cheese) with pineapple chunks or late bedtimes or sassing. Mother had to prepare us for futures and careers and responsibilities later in life, but Baby Sugar was just Baby Sugar. Any indulgence was not just acceptable, it was encouraged, and the little dog quickly became the spoiled child Mother would never have and Dad would never have wanted.

When we moved from Ohio, Mother carried her shaggy, aging canine on her lap all the way down to Miami, even when it was her turn to drive The Old Chevy. We tended to name things we loved, like The Old Chevy. For the record, with Baby Sugar behind the wheel, Joe and I counted more than thirty carloads of people out on the highway who did double takes, thinking there was a dog behind the wheel. And every time they stared, Joe and I whooped with glee.

"For Pete's sake, Isabel," my father would plead when Mother and Baby Sugar drove, "put that dog in the back with the kids while I try to get some shuteye. She'll be fine back there." But Baby Sugar liked driving or riding shotgun or reading the map, not sitting in the back like some know-nothing kid, and she retained her front-seat rights all day, every day. The nights, however, presented a problem.

"Excuse me, sir," Mother would begin to the owner when we stopped at an auto court and the sign read NO PETS, "but we have this little pup who will be so afraid if she can't come into our room tonight. I don't suppose you could make an exception for a well-trained pure bred, could you?" Baby Sugar would look up, trying to look like the well-trained pure bred she wasn't. Knowing there was no such animal in our party, I also would look up, just to see the owner's reaction, and noticed the owners generally were more interested in Mother than in the dog.

No slip into dialect to detract from the practiced phrase. A dazzling smile and bright blue eyes, Mother's not

Baby Sugar's, helped the case more than a little, so one night I decided to try the flirtatiousness-for-gain method myself.

"Excuse me, Sir, do you have a playground set for us?" I interjected. Dazzling smile. Bright blue eyes. No response, nothing. Except for Joe, who noted every detail of the exchange and reenacted my pathetic attempt to anyone and everyone he encountered in the free world for at least a year following the trip.

Horridly embarrassed over Mother's fuss about the dog, Dad would keep as far away from the scene as possible. We could hear him coughing and shuffling and getting into the trunk and struggling with suitcases, trying to appear much too busy to deal with registering the family for the night. I sometimes wondered if Dad was more than a little jealous of the huge amount of Mother's sugar that Baby Sugar cheated him out of, but I knew better than to mention the slight foot assistance that Dad regularly offered Baby Sugar's rear end when she, Baby Sugar, that is, not Mother, walked by.

"You know we have a AAA rating, ma'am," a typical auto court owner would explain, "and we don't want to jeopardize that, but I guess we can make an exception for a well-trained, pure-bred, uh, miniature sheepdog, or is she a cocker spaniel?"

"Oh, thank you!" Mother would gush and smile, ignoring the question about doggy heritage.

You've probably known women like my mother who spoil their little dogs, but I doubt any of them were Pennsylvania Dutch women, the women who spent most of their lives cleaning their houses, hanging and ironing laundry, cooking dishes from the old country, and shunning people they were mad at. Such an extreme demonstration of affection, especially toward a germ-carrying, hair-losing, mouth-slobbering, add-nothing-to-the-income pet, was more than unusual.

When we finally arrived in Miami, there were two

criteria for a rental house. The first criterion, of course, was that it had to be a certified, Pennsylvania Dutch-approved, sanitized, sterilized, and ideally Sanforized dwelling. The second criterion was acceptance of a small dog. A sugar dog. But our landlord had no problem with a pet in the house. In fact, he bragged that he had even raised a bottle-fed goat in his bathroom for a whole month until she got a good start in life. I knew this to be true since I'd already seen a large nanny goat tied out back with a toilet seat around her neck.

"My wife likes goat milk," the landlord explained, "and old Pansy Sue, the goat, that is, not the missus, tries to turn around and butt me when I milk her. The toilet seat keeps her from doin' that."

We rented the little cottage and settled in to our first years in Miami, Mother finding delight in the ceaseless sunshine where she could hang wash outside winter and summer. No more cold trips to a frosty basement and hoisting half-frozen clothes back upstairs. No more mud and slush tracked into the kitchen by children needing to warm up by the furnace. Baby Sugar spent most of her days out of doors, celebrating her new freedom in the cheerful glow of the back yard, where there were new holes to dig in a new yard and a goat next door to torment. She only came in at night, unless, of course, she felt the need to be with her mistress. Baby Sugar, that is, not Mother.

But idyllic times, even for sugar dogs, have ways of evolving into glory and self importance and hubris, and, of course, ending in tragedy. The loss of Baby Sugar was a disrupting time in our household, and we later found ourselves marking time in relation to the day Baby Sugar drove off, just like other folks marked time from Pearl Harbor or the day President Roosevelt died.

"It was the April after Baby Sugar drove off...."

"About a year before Baby Sugar drove off, no, more like

a year and a half...."

"We had just celebrated the dog's ninth birthday when she began having some most disturbing symptoms. Incidentally, Joe was also having some most disturbing symptoms. Baby Sugar coughed, wouldn't eat, and slept a lot. Joe coughed, sneezed, slept a lot, and dabbed at his watering eyes with one of Dad's huge white handkerchiefs. Mother knew Baby Sugar needed to see a veterinarian, a totally unheard of luxury in our days of thrift and saving and sacrifice, and after several weeks of observation, it was finally decided that Baby Sugar looked and acted so sick that the veterinarian money would just have to come out of the budget. Then we'd see about Joe's unusual health status. First things first.

Early the next morning Mother dressed in one of her most plain housedresses, hid her diamond engagement ring and gold watch under the mattress, instructed us to put on some older play clothes, forego our sandals, and leave our hair a little *struwli* (uncombed) in the back. This shabby appearance was supposed to convince the veterinarian that we were among the dirt poor of South Florida, and ideally he'd go easy on the bill. As we drove to the South Dade Small Animal Hospital, Baby Sugar was so sick that she had to be held up in her standard front seat position by the coughing, sneezing, watering Joe.

The waiting room of the South Dade Small Animal Hospital was full of howling and hissing, slipping and sliding house pets being restrained by owners of varying degrees of patience. If this is the South Dade Small Animal Hospital, I wondered, what would the cut-off be? Would a Great Dane be denied service here? An alligator? A peacock? Also, would they move the darkest-colored animals to a back waiting room like they did at our own doctor's office? I hoped not. That practice seemed to upset Mother, and it wasn't a good day to get her more riled up.

I was jolted back into reality when a nurse called out, "Baby Sugar Malone." Joe and I followed Mother as she carried her dog to the examining room and put her on the stainless steel table. The veterinarian gave her a good going over. Baby Sugar, that is, not Mother. The diagnosis: Baby Sugar had many problems, mostly associated with aging. He felt it best to "put her down," as he phrased it.

"And, by the way," the veterinarian mentioned, "your boy may be allergic to animals, with all that sneezing and watering. Maybe you should have him tested."

"First things first," Mother replied. She paid the bill of two dollars. The nurse had mentioned five dollars was the usual fee, so I knew our disguise had worked, and I knew the discount visit would help Mother's mood a little. I wondered if I could pull off this same shabbiness-for-greed hoax when I next needed a wrapped marshmallow cookie from Mr. Potter's corner store, but remembering my disastrous encounter with the auto court owner, put the thought out of my head.

After a lengthy discussion with my father, one which included the possibility of Joe's having an allergy to dogs, it was decided that Baby Sugar would go to doggy heaven. The problem was, no one was willing to take her back to the veterinarian for the final rites.

"I can't take her," Mother whispered.

"I can't take her," Dad responded, probably feeling guilty about his rear-end assists.

"I can't take her," the landlord explained, "I'm just too soft hearted."

"I can't take her," the landlord's wife added, "I don't drive."

"I can't take her," Mr. P.K. Tucker told us. "You'd never look at me the same again."

I felt it wise not to mention that it might be a good

thing if we didn't look at Mr. P. K. Tucker the same again, what with that stubby little sixth finger on his left hand.

"I can't take her," Mrs. P.K. Tucker whimpered, "but you can use my phone to make the arrangements."

"What arrangements?" Mother asked. "The vet said just drop her off. We don't need an appointment."

"Well, I was thinkin'," Mrs. P.K. Tucker explained, "why don't you jus' send her in a taxi cab? You know how she likes to ride up front of a car."

"Have the cab driver, do you mean, just take her to the vet and leave her?" Mother was digesting the concept. "That's just too peculiar," she responded.

"And it would cost money," Joe reminded her as he finished a ten-in-a-row sneezing fit. I complimented him on his new record, and he appreciated the acknowledgment.

"Well, jus' call and see how much it would cost," Mrs. P.K. Tucker suggested.

Which is what I mentioned earlier. The man at the cab company yelled into the phone, "You want me to take yer dog where to do what?"

"Don't make me say it, please, again," Mother appealed to the man on the other end. "How much it would cost to, down to the South Dade Small Animal Hospital, take her. One way trip."

"Let's see, ma'am, if I understand what you said, you want me to take yer dog to the South Dade Small Animal Hospital and leave 'er there. That'd be one dollar and fifty-five cents."

"Mother covered the mouthpiece of the phone and repeated what the cab man said. Joe did a quick arithmetic, arriving at three dollars and fifty-five cents for the entire procedure, including vet bill.

"Please send a cab over as soon as possible, Sir," she

whispered.

Mother's Pennsylvania Dutch frugality snapped in again, and she fretted over which old blanket should be used for Baby Sugar. It was silly to waste a perfectly good blanket that was only fifteen or twenty years old on a dog, but Mother eventually found one bad enough to justify the loss from our aging linen stock, and wrapped Baby Sugar in it. We all cooed our goodbyes. It was easy to let a sick animal stop suffering. Even Mother agreed with that.

When the taxi arrived, Mother explained to the driver that Baby Sugar liked to sit up front and help drive. Silently, the bewildered driver opened the front door. By this time, nothing seemed to surprise him, and he climbed back into the cab and sat behind the wheel. Mother positioned Baby Sugar next to him, propping her up in the blanket and positioning a piece from a torn road map up on the dash where she could help navigate. Dad, struggling to compute the tip on the grotesque taxi trip, finally handed the driver four dollars to cover everything and to buy himself a beer to help forget the whole incident.

The last time we saw Baby Sugar, she was happily driving down SW 42nd Terrace, looking like the magnificent, map-reading, car-driving, well-trained, pure-bred mongrel she was.

"Come on back to the Tucker's house," Dad called out to everyone. "We have to make an appointment for Joe to see the doctor." First things first.

14

Chapter 3

"...the sound of silence."

- Paul Simon

Can you think back to the middle of the 20th century, or have you heard tales of towns where you didn't lock the doors at night, and where you knew everyone for several blocks around by name, and what the man of the house did for a living, and how the woman of the house managed her family's life? If you can, then add suburban Miami to the list of those towns.

Miami. It was a wonderful place to live back in the 1940s and 50s. It really did look like the picture post cards the sunburned tourists bought down at Rexall Drugs and sent back home to the folks Up North. Beaches with sand so white it hurt your eyes to look. Palm trees, some of them bent so far over from the off shore wind that you could walk up the trunks if you hung on with both hands and feet like Jimmy the baby monkey at the Monkey Jungle over near the Dixie Highway. And waves you could jump for hours until your father gave his final command to come out of the water now or you'd really be in trouble this time.

West of Miami was the Everglades, where Seminole women sat in their open chickee huts, hunched over Singer treadle sewing machine, stitching strips of colored fabric into huge shirts and skirts which billowed out for air circulation while providing protection from the mosquitoes that swarmed in any shady spot. I thought the colorful clothes made the Seminoles look like walking rainbows, and took Walking Rainbow as my native name when we played cowboys and Indians, even though Joe informed me a rainbow could never walk. He did concede it sometimes seemed to move as we drove through the swamp, though.

After World War II, Miami boasted some of the more amazing attractions in Florida. The Parrot Jungle was a place I only allowed myself to be taken once—it frightened a little girl pretty well as the huge birds swooshed their long, strong wings, flying in a most unnatural looking, nearly standing-up position. How my mother allowed several parrots to land on her extended arms and the top of her head, making her look like some ornithological Carmen Miranda, was as foreign to me as the Cuban language. I hid safely behind my father as he snapped a picture of the ghastly event and declined viewing the photo more than once when it came back from the drug store.

Vizcaya Palace and Art Museum was far more little-girl friendly. It had no scary birds, and it had enough nudes to fill in the gaps in my immature understanding of anatomy. The Venetian Pool had coral rock caves where you could swim in and out and pretend you were Tarzan, or in my case, Jane. And, of course, the alligators were wrestled at the places where the sunburned tourists stopped on their way out of town.

Some folks said Miami was just New York, South, and maybe that was true if you lived over on The Beach—Miami Beach, where the lady lying next to you on a blanket may have a tattoo on her forearm from a German concentration camp. But we lived out in the vast southwest section in one of the developments that was built after the war. The Big War, Dad called it. He said the houses seemed to spring up overnight, just like the string beans Mother planted every spring on the south side of the house. Most of the newer houses were white with white tile roofs to reflect the sun. In shady Coral Gables, many of the houses looked like pink Spanish villas with grandiose

16

banyan trees and old, established shrubbery to help keep them cool.

About a year after Baby Sugar drove away, we bought our own house at the corner of 58th Avenue and 38th Court. The house itself was unspectacular, other than being a CBS—cement block structure—differentiating it from the frame houses that tended to blow away during hurricanes. It faced that back dirt driveway to the local millionaire's mansion, and sat centered on two building lots like a wide, old woman, forever watching across the street and dreaming of what could have been.

The house was a lot like our family. We were generally, as the saying goes, big fish in small ponds, but always with the larger ponds close enough by to remind us of our true station.

Elevated on three rows of cement block foundation and widened with a screened Florida Room which joined the living room to the garage, our house was larger than the others in the development, with the additional size and acreage being either a luxury or a nuisance, depending on who was admiring it and who was cleaning, mowing, and weeding it. I have no idea how many other families this house has sheltered, but my strong attachment for it assures me we were the house's true family. We planted the mahogany seeds that grew into shady Goliaths, and we hand-dug the swimming pool that provided years of enjoyment. I'm told the house still wears our personality, but actually, it's the other way around: The house helped shape our family's personality.

It was a tough job, even for a six year old, but by using a combination dragging-bumping technique, I was able to move my heavy rocking chair out to the sidewalk. There I could see all the way down the next long block and watch the cars speeding by on Bird Road, where the bus would pick us up for the first

17

day of school. My mother and brother Joe had warned me I'd have a long wait—it was nowhere near time to begin the walk up to the bus stop, but feeling elegant with my braids pinned up over my head and wearing my red sundress, the one I could pull down over my shoulders if no one was looking, I was content to wait and to rock and to squeak and to watch. Besides, it gave me time to think over the bedroom possibilities again.

Even though we'd been in the new house a few weeks, it was understood the middle-sized bedroom would not officially be rewarded to either my brother or me until after the new baby came, and the award would depend on whether the new baby were a boy or a girl. As the monkey-do half of the monkey-see/monkey-do relationship with my brother, I'd been wishing very hard for a sister, my ticket to the bigger bedroom, mostly because Joe said he'd been wishing for a brother—there is a natural logic to these things. Well, we'd know soon enough—the baby was due, whatever that meant, any day. I turned my attention back to rocking and to admiring my new shoes, and to watching that spot where the bus would come and take me to my new world.

Since I managed to get the heady, dew covered, late summer roses my mother had wrapped in waxed paper to my teacher, and since I managed not to lose my hot lunch quarter, I considered that first day of first grade a success. And success was in the air. Like spent horses returning to the stable, Joe and I ran into the cool house from the bus stop a few weeks later to find we had a new sister, Faith Rose. I'd won the prize—the bigger bedroom. I couldn't help feeling sorry for Joe—he was stuck with a room by himself, and it was the smallest in the house. I did have to admire him, however, for the poise with which he accepted his defeat. He even managed to keep a wide smile on his face.

The bedrooms were quickly decorated, at least that's what my mother fancied it. From the depths of her Pennsylvania

Dutch austerity surfaced her decorating technique: a few sticks of utilitarian furniture and one or two knickknacks *chust for pretty.* My bedroom held Faith's crib, my bed, a dresser, bathinette and all its hoses, and a toy box, all pulled together with a bubble gum pink rug. Even I, the blissful, don't-anyone-ever-forget-it winner of the bigger bedroom, noticed the extra baby furniture took up a lot of room. I don't think I'd really given much thought to any additional people or furniture in the room, only to the possibility of permanent ownership. Mother reminded me, "You chust can't have it all," meaning I had to take the bad part of the bigger bedroom—all the extra furniture and a howling infant—along with the good part, being the victor.

Shortly after Baby Sugar had driven off, Joe was diagnosed with some major allergies, dust being one of them, so carpeting was out of the question in his bedroom. Instead, he was able to pick out wall-to-wall linoleum which could be mopped frequently. He chose an energetic pattern of cowboys and Indians, which were either chasing or being chased—depending on which pattern row you followed—over a background which did look surprisingly like what desert sand must look like. But the Western motif was modified by the bedspread Mother had received as a wedding gift ten years earlier and had saved in her cedar chest. Woven of heavy cotton and reversible, it sported either maroon dogs on an ivory background or ivory dogs on a maroon background, depending on which side you looked at. I think the plan had originally been to feature an authentic Indian headdress, a souvenir from a trip to Arizona, by tacking it up on the wall of the bedroom, but due to the dust allergy—sneeze, sneeze, sneeze—Mother's artistic flair had to be curtailed. The gaudy souvenir was stashed in a paper bag and tossed up into the attic, and Mother tacked a calendar from Wilson's Funeral Home up on the wall instead. Somehow, it seemed appropriate, what with the impending linoleum cowboy-

Indian war casualties. Wall decoration having been completed, we turned our attention back to a long morning of furniture arrangement.

"We can't leave it so," Mother realized after trying to arrange Joe's room while simultaneously tending the baby. She saw that Joe's workbench was against a wall with no electrical outlet. "It wonders me how I forget. Sometimes I do *dappi* (act clumsy), but the *hutschi* (little ponies) look good, *blotzing* (jumping) around the desert on the linoleum." Mikey LeRoy Smithson, Joe's new best friend, was in the project with us. He developed a quizzical look on his face, excused himself to Mother, and went home. It was later reported that he told his grandmother he thought Mother was talking in tongues like at the Baptist tent revival, and he wanted to get out before someone asked him to accept Jesus as his Savior.

Joe had a twin bed, a small desk, and his workbench, which was really just a door on four legs. There he kept his gizmos. Gizmos, I was told were important small pieces of metal and wire and wood, all very necessary for Joe's impressive building and electrical and chemical experiments. In reality, Joe's gizmos were generally things he didn't want to put away on cleaning day. Mother respected Joe's experiments so much that she did not question the gizmos or make him keep them organized like a true Pennsylvania Dutchman would have arranged his workbench.

The workbench was usually cluttered with *Boys Life* magazines and wadded up notebook paper and laundry of questionable age. As I struggled to keep my crowded room Mother-approved-tidy like a true Pennsylvania Dutch woman-in-training, I'd sit on the floor, sorting a pile of toys and books and call out loudly, "A *Boys Life* magazine isn't a gizmo." It didn't take long to learn that boys were encouraged in their ingenious projects, be they electrical, chemical, or organizational, and girls were encouraged to come behind and *redd up* (clean up) the messes.

Even with the untidy workbench, Joe's room seemed large and inviting. With all of his furniture pushed back against the walls, there was even room for entertaining, an impossibility in my room because of the baby's sleeping or crying, especially the crying. The crying, crying, crying.

Eventually Faith Rose and I became compatible roommates, and it was hard to remember those first difficult years together. As the months passed, I'd lie in bed and watch her finally drift off to sleep, curled like a kitten in the warm breeze beneath the white curtains that puffed out like starched cotton clouds with every breath of air, and I'd wonder if our beautiful baby would someday question the meanings of her names as I had mine.

Chapter 4

"Of thine ankle lightly turn'd,
With those beauties, scarce discern'd, . . .
Like twin water lilies, born,
In the coolness of the morn."

- John Keats

If you walked from our house up to the corner of Bird Road and Red Road, you'd soon arrive at the little shopping center that served the residential area—Holly's Five and Dime, B-Thrifty groceries, Rexall Drugs, and the Texaco station. This Texaco station was Dad's favorite filling station, but I'd ridden in the car with him to many others and was always impressed with his routine: stop the engine, pull on the emergency brake, stick his head out of the window, and call out, "Fill 'er up with ethyl, Mack."

Ethel and Mack, I mused. They must be married, or maybe they just work together. But when do they put Ethel in the car? I'd never seen her—no smartly uniformed woman ever showed up.

Although very proud of my father's close association with gas station attendants everywhere and his knowing all of them by their first names, coincidentally Mack, when I began reading, I couldn't figure out why all those Macks had on someone else's uniform. Sometimes the colorfully embroidered name patches read, Bud or Bill or Sam. You'd think the oil companies would watch out for such blatant infractions.

Hanging out a back window and watching Dad supervise

the windshield wipe, the oil check, the water check, the tire kick, and the gas pumping into The Old Chevy, I grinned and waved at the attendant, trying to catch his eye, seeking my due recognition as the daughter of the man who knew everyone by name.

"Dad sure knows a lot of Macks," I informed Joe.

"Whaddaya mean?" he asked.

Feeling superior at being able to report a remarkable event to my brother, I continued, "Dad knows all the gas station men and their names are Mack."

"Their names aren't all Mack," Joe informed me. "That's just a nickname he uses. They call each other Mick or Mack in Ohio because they're Irish."

Realizing neither Dad nor I deserved any tribute for his now obviously average communicative skills, I quickly ducked my head back into the car. I'd been betrayed. This man had led me to believe he knew everyone's name and had let me grin like a monkey at the busy attendants.

"Sometimes, Mercy," Joe began in his older brother lecture style, "I wonder what goes on in your head."

"Well what about Ethel?" I continued.

"What about ethyl?"

"Well, where is she? How comes she never comes out? She's supposed to fill something up, but I've never seen her," I explained.

"My Great Aunt Mule!" Joe exploded in one of his favorite expressions, "Ethyl is just gas. It's a good gas. It's not regular gas. The Old Chevy can't take regular anymore. You're kidding me, aren't you?"

"Yeah," I answered quietly. "I was just kidding. Heh, heh, heh."

Dad got back in the car and headed over to Rexall Drugs to pick up a pint of ice cream for a cool summer surprise.

24

"Good evening, Murleen," he greeted the lady behind the soda fountain. "We'd like a pint of vanilla to take home."

"Evening, Mr. Malone. Evening kids. Ya sure ya jus want a pint? Aren't there five a ya?" she asked helpfully.

"Yes, but the baby doesn't eat it, and Mrs. Malone only eats a little." I realized Dad was getting uncomfortable with himself for explaining the purchase.

"Well, here ya go. Enjoy it, y'all." Murleen tucked a loose blond curl into her hairnet and accepted the twenty cents, and we climbed back into the car and drove home.

No matter what Murleen thought, I knew ice cream was a special treat, what with the new baby and the new house and furniture. At home we poured bubbling root beer over the small scoops of vanilla, and it actually stretched nicely into four Boston coolers.

"Why do they call them Boston coolers if we live in Miami?" I inquired.

"They just started there," Joe advised.

Continuing my observations while sipping the heavenly drink and trying not to let the bubbles pop near my nose, I began disseminating information about the lady at the drug store.

"Murleen Rexall wanted to sell us more ice cream, Mom, but Dad said one pint was enough."

"Who?" Mother inquired.

"You know, Murleen Rexall."

"I know Murleen, but her last name isn't Rexall."

"Yes, it is. Her name's stitched on her dress—Murleen Rexall. Like her sister, Lurleen Rexall," I explained.

"My Great-Great Aunt Mule!" Joe exploded.

"Rexall just means she works there, Mercy. It's not her last name," Mother gently assured me.

This was too much for one night. First the Macks, then

the Ethels, now the Rexalls.

Dad, who'd only been half listening, laughed and spit a mouthful of cooler across the table. "That's a good name, Mercy," he said while wiping up his mouth and the tablecloth, "Murleen Rexall and Lurleen Rexall—the Rexalls."

From then on that's how they were known around our house.

Murleen and Lurleen Rexall were twins, though not identical. They must have been close to thirty when we moved in, and one or the other worked the soda fountain shifts at the drug store. The twins were large, attractive, buxom women— very healthy looking—and obviously had flourished during their growing up years on the farm in the middle of the state. Friendly, helpful, and congenial, Mother described them as "good as gold." They were both brunettes, although prone to peroxide bottles, which they got at discount at the drug store. Their eyebrows were still black and were plucked into a surprised look like Jerry Colonna, except they didn't wiggle them around like he did. Murleen and Lurleen had the hands of men. Their large, meaty fingers were like the sausages we saw in the Jewish delicatessen cold case in Coral Gables, and they'd pound the index finger on the counter to make a point or just to have something to do with a restless hand.

"Don't you never talk to me about them hoods—thumb, thump, thump—them JDs—juvenile delinquents—thump, thump, thump—just oughta get a good spankin', and then we'll be seein' who takes a car joy ridin'—thump, thump, thump."

Joe and I went up to the drug store often, usually with two big, empty pop bottles to trade in on fudge-cicles. Because of their striking similarities, and because I'd had no prior contact with twins, Murleen and Lurleen quickly lost their individual identities to me, and I considered them one entity—The Rexalls. "Well, come on back, kids," one or the other would command, "I see ya both got Seh-MUPP bottles with ya." Looking at the labels on the bottles, we decided the current Rexall was probably referring to what we called 7-Up, and quickly put them on the counter for our nickels.

Sometimes we chose fountain Cokes instead of fudge-cicles, and sitting on a swiveling stool at the long linoleum-topped counter, I could examine every detail of the Rexalls' workplace while Joe only worked on his drink.

A large paddle fan turned slowly over the Rexalls as they worked, and mirrors covered the wall behind the counter, allowing me both to study the fountain details and to watch myself make charming faces when Joe wasn't looking. There were seven seats at the counter and four booths across from it. The twins stood on a wooden, lattice-type platform. Joe said it was for foot relief, wood being softer to walk on than cement, but I worried about what fell between the slats. I shouldn't have. The twins kept the fountain area immaculate, and I'm sure they hoisted the slats at the end of the day, sweeping out any scrap of bread or lettuce or meatloaf.

There was a magnificent three-cup milkshake machine at one end of the shelf below the mirror, a big toaster at the other end, and three cake plates on pedestals between the two—one for cake, one for pie, one for donuts. Between every two seats at the counter were shiny metal cages which had separate spots for the menu, the salt and pepper shakers, the napkins, and the straws. The Rexalls didn't worry about kids playing with the straws. One too many and they'd come up, look you in the face, and thump. Thump, thump. There were seldom second infractions, although the temptation to shoot a wrapper across the counter sometimes was irresistible.

There were colorful signs for Holsum bread, Hershey's

Chocolate, and Chase and Sanborn coffee pasted up on the mirror, as well as a sign for the lunch and dinner specials. All-in-all, a cheerful place, and a joy for a child as in love with cash registers and professional waitresses as I to observe.

Hmm. Pork salad sandwich for lunch with potato chips and a drink. Thiry-five cents. Roast turkey with mashed potatoes and gravy and cranberry sauce for dinner. Fifty-five cents. And you get a roll with it. Maybe we could go out to dinner here sometime, I thought. We could feed the whole family for, uhh, two dollars and twenty cents. Faith would share my plate.

The cardboard Coca Cola poster boy's eyes followed you around the store, no matter where you went, just like the picture of Jesus in the gold frame over at Holly's Five and Dime. The poster was in a frame on the wall rather than on the mirror, and some neighborhood children, not I, of course, wondered if it really was Mr. Johnson, the pharmacist, peering out, monitoring the fountain operations and how much whipped cream the Rexalls put on the shakes.

Sitting at the fountain for long periods of time, we heard a lot of gossip, not the least of which the Rexalls shared themselves as they overlapped on the lunch shift.

"How'd yer date go?" Murleen asked her sister. "I didn't hear ya come in last night."

"Oh, it was fun. Blackie's such a big shot over to the hall. He's the head Bingo caller now, you know."

"Well, that's wonderful," Murleen conceded.

Blackie, known more formally around the fountain as Blackie the One Eyed Bingo Caller, was Lurleen's long-time boyfriend. Murleen dated lots of men from what we could gather, but Lurleen was true to Blackie, who had lost the eye in that unfortunate alligator wrestling accident, and now sported a pirate's patch over the hole.

"Ya," Lurleen continued, "He lets me sit up at the table with him and put the Bingo balls back in the drum, and he let me talk into the microphone last night."

"No! What'd ya say? Weren't ya scared? How'd ya sound?"

"Oh, I just said, 'Hello, I'm Lurleen, and I'm happy to be here with you tonight.'"

"Very professional," Murleen judged as she nodded at the quality of the speech—thump, thump, thump. "Well, let a person know when yer gonna be late. I worry and can't sleep and ya know I gotta be here at six to start the coffee."

"Oh, I know. I'm sorry, but Blackie 'n the boys just started tellin' the jokes 'n I couldn't get 'em to leave, we was laughin' so hard...," Lurleen explained as she winked at Murleen and nodded at Joe and me, indicating she'd repeat the jokes at a later time.

"That's okay, Sis, I just worry about ya, but that's real good about the microphone." Murleen ended the topic with a gentle hug with her now nearly famous sister. "Wouldn't Mama be proud," she added.

I found the Rexalls' uniforms incredibly glamorous and could recite every inch of them, head to toe. Thick brown hairnet over blondish hair. Starched headband, like the front of a nurse's cap, only smaller and pinned to cover the beginning of the hairnet. Turquoise nylon dress with white collar and cuffs, and, of course, their names embroidered on the left breast pocket from which a stiff, white, tatted and embroidered handkerchief protruded like a frozen linen orchid. White apron with two deep pockets in which they kept an order pad, pen, lipstick for quick and frequent repairs, and their tips. No nylons in the summer. White nylons in the winter, even though Nurse Ada Lynn at Dr. Proctor's office had told them white nylons were for nurses only, thank you very much.

The glamour of the uniform ended at the hemline—it did not go down to their shoes, which, due to the size of the feet, were huge, white, thick-soled, laced-up monsters. Lucky for them, I thought, you have to peek over the counter to see the shoes, and I was probably the only one who did, and then was always sorry. I felt the shoes were too much of a contrast with the chic uniform, and probably white high heels would have been better.

I saw the Rexalls frequently for several years, and they were always dressed in the turquoise and white uniforms, so I assumed they, like our priest at church, wore the official garb, day and night, function to function. I couldn't imagine the twins or Father Carroll in pajamas, shorts, or, God forbid, a bathing suit, so it came as a great surprise when I nearly bumped into Lurleen in B-Thrifty's one day. She was grocery shopping and wearing a summer dress and sneakers as big as my dad's. With her hair out of the hairnet, I didn't recognize her. I did a quick double take, finally placed her, and ducked behind the rack of Holsum bread and donuts so she couldn't see me. Afraid of what Mr. Peterson would say if he knew she was both AWOL from the drug store and out of uniform, I put the *Archie* comic book back in the magazine stand and left, vowing never to mention it to anyone, even under interrogation. I wouldn't want to be the one whose testimony would convict her.

But it got worse. We'd gone to the double feature at the LeJune Drive-In, and on Mother's and my trip back from the restroom at intermission, we bumped into both Rexalls. They were out of uniform, but odder still, were dressed identically, just like little girl twins. Red bowling shirts, black shorts, patent leather belts, and huge white wedgie sandals. Their hair hung down to their shoulders and was a study in color bands, graduating from the black roots through the various shades of brown and blond to the platinum tips.

30

"Good evening, Murleen, Lurleen," Mother remarked. "Nice night for a movie."

The Rexalls spoke either concurrently or in spurts, finishing each other's phrases.

MURLEEN and LURLEEN: "Well, hey, Ms. Malone. Hey, Mercy."

MURLEEN: "Nice night for a . . ."

LURLEEN: "Movie."

MURLEEN: "Don't cha just love . . ."

LURLEEN: "Donald O'Connor? Isn't that mule a . . ."

MURLEEN: "Kick. No pun . . ."

LURLEEN: "Intended. Haw. Haw."

Mother looked at me and smiled. I was standing there with my jaw on my chest.

The newsreel that night had a brief tribute to Eng and Chang Bunker, the famous Siamese twins—it was the eightieth anniversary of their deaths. I couldn't help but make the connection.

Later, as I lay in bed, I envisioned the Rexalls in a newsreel on TV. They'd be at the drug store and in their uniforms, but you couldn't see their shoes. I'd be interviewing them and asking leading questions about being twins and making up double chocolate shakes and hamburger platters. Then they'd be in identical outfits—sweaters and poodle skirts and saddle shoes would be nice, if they made them that big. They'd be at the Bingo hall, and Blackie would adjust his eye patch and ask them to say a few words into the microphone.

Their mama would be so proud.

31

Chapter 5

"To us the ashes of our ancestors are sacred. . . ."
- Chief Seattle

The Grace part of my name didn't just fall out of thin air. I'd already been told many times that the oldest girl always had it as her middle name. My grandmother first chronicled the list of Graces one day when she, as the Pennsylvania Dutch term goes, redded up the bed she used when visiting from Up North.

We tugged on sheets, and she began, "You are Mercedes Grace. Your mother is Isabel Grace. I am Margaret Grace. Here, toss me the pillow, Snickle Fritz. My mother was Caroline Grace. Her mother was Anna Grace . . ." Having only sketchy visions of old women in a musty photo album, I could not assimilate much—the names just seemed to go on and on and on.

The litany was repeated often, both by Grandma and Mother, and I gladly took in the information a little at a time, digesting small pieces. I'd listen to each story individually and master it, and when I was ready, would ask for more. Although the Graces gave me a sense of importance as the youngest installment of a great plan, I also wanted to know about the other family members.

My grandmother would tell lengthy stories about everyone she could remember, except her son John. There she would stop and say nothing. Although I had just fleeting recollections about Uncle John, one was disturbing. I was probably only three or four at the time, and I remembered him being very small and very dark. We were standing in my grandmother's dining room, and he was shouting at my weeping mother.

No one talked about Uncle John, and no one would tell me anything about him. Once I set up my young Aunt Edna, and like a persistent salesman, kept my foot in the door until she weakened. But like the others, Aunt Edna was skilled at avoiding the issue, so I had to withdraw my foot until I could swindle information from another unwilling customer.

Joe did remember seeing Uncle John often for about a year when we were really little and still in Ohio. He said he was very small, just like I remembered, and, yes, he did have black hair. Joe remembered he was very nice to us little children, but seemed always to be fighting with his mother and sisters. Then he was gone. That was all.

My suspicion was that Uncle John had been a Nazi spy, and I frequently looked in the newspaper for articles about a John Kramer, former Nazi spy, from Niles, Ohio. I imagined he was in prison, serving a life sentence or had been hanged from the neck until dead, or maybe even electrocuted like Julius Rosenberg, but Rachel, one of my Jewish friends, said he was probably hiding in Argentina with Eichmann. I imagined Uncle John in a small toreador outfit, dodging bulls and police, and trying to learn Spanish. "Donde esta el bullo?" he'd inquire.

If Uncle John added a sense of intrigue, I always found simple comfort and support from the Graces who preceded me, as if they watched over, making me feel I was no longer on my own. Over the years, I'd regularly implore a busy mother or a less busy grandmother, "Tell me about the Graces," until eventually I could recite their histories and the histories of each of their families. I listened, internalized, and drew great strength for my own body and soul. I was no longer just a middle child—a child who often felt her accomplishments weren't so important as her older brother's, nor her needs so great as her younger sister's, nor her wants so deserving as either of theirs.

It wasn't until I was nearly grown that I learned the truth about Uncle John, and although I'd regularly pondered over him and my other ancestors throughout my growing-up years, for the most part I lived my life in the present, like any other kid, except, of course, I was a Grace.

Chapter 6

*"The world's a theater, the earth a stage
Which God and Nature do with actors fill."*
- Thomas Heywood

Dear Gramma,

How are you? I am fine. We had a circis and Faith and I put on shows for the family on Friday nit and we had so many acts that Daddy told us the adence had to go to bed and he wood give us 10¢ to quite becas he was tird. We had hawhyn girls and made hula skrts out of papr bags and cut them to look like gras and tap dans and balla danse and cowgirls and magick and bathng butes. And singrs and circis bear back ridr and Faith rode me around the livnroom. The gave us 5 ¢ to see the show each but Joe wanted his nicl back. I have been haning from the swng set to stretch and be taler so I am not shortst in my clas. Joe says it is dum but I thin I am taler all redy. I have to go now becos Faith is tring to color on this papr look clos you can see but she is cute. Love and ksses and tell Aunt Edna hey. Mercy

P.S. I love you.

P.S. Whn will you vist agan?

X x x x x o o o o o o o o o o

P.S. S.S. I mis you very much ! ! ! ! ! !

P.S.S.S.S. I hope Uncle John dosnt get hurt by bulls.

Chapter 7

"Well, I feel a bit tired.
It's been a long day.
The garden party, a dinner party, and the opera!
Rather too much of a good thing."
- George Bernard Shaw

You have to remember that Pennsylvania Dutch thing about my mother.

Imagine a life spent cleaning and organizing and saving and re-cleaning and re-organizing and saving more, and, oh yes, teaching school up north before Joe and I were born. A life represented in microcosm by her daily chore of cutting the backs off used envelopes to make paper for lists so that she wouldn't forget an upcoming cleaning or reorganization activity.

You have to remember this if you are going to understand about Bertha.

"Hurry up, Mercy, Mrs. James just called and wants us to come early to help. Joe, Faith, hurry up. We've got to go early."

"Great," I thought, "We get to go to the party early." I had been looking forward to the event for weeks, ever since Mrs. James had called and said she was throwing her granddaughter Kathy Jo Lynn a huge birthday celebration. Weekly updates for the extravaganza generated our code name for the event, Bertha's Big Blow Out. Nothing would be too expensive, and no activity too much trouble. Even pony rides. We kids couldn't wait.

"Bigger," Mrs. James had said, "than that smarty pants Wanda Conklin done give her grandson Earl Dean." Even though I was only seven, I knew the element of competition with a rival would ensure a better party for us kids.

Mr. and Mrs. James, Roy and Bertha, owned the rental house we'd occupied a few years earlier, and we enjoyed going back to visit them, especially if their granddaughter Kathy Jo Lynn was there. Because they lived next door, Roy was able to paint and shingle and nail boards back on our house as they blew off during hurricanes, but he and Bertha spent virtually no time on their own place. Because the Jameses had been so good to our family, and because Mother was a proper young woman, she pretended not to notice the mess over at Bertha and Roy's. Spoiling all of us with food and toys and roses seemed to please them, and we loved their attention and friendship.

Bertha James was very slight, and when she sat on the couch, which was nearly always, she slouched on her mid back rather than her bottom with her legs way out front, generating an exhausted appearance. She had salt-and-pepper graying hair, and the skin on her upper arms hung like draperies from her shoulders. Her main daily activity was writing to the little *Miami Gazette* newspaper. She wrote to the editor, to the advice-to-the-lovelorn column, and to the happy homemaker. Fortunately the *Gazette* was a small paper and appreciative of the letters Bertha or anyone else sent in. From what we could tell, they printed all of hers. This did not leave a lot of time for the mundane chores of housekeeping. As Bertha said, she was more of a career woman than a maid.

But when Bertha found out Mother was expecting a baby, she would lurk around the kitchen of our little rental house every Monday morning until the wet laundry was in the basket. Then she'd find Roy and tell him to carry the laundry out back and hang it on the line. "You don't want the apple to drop before its time," she'd explain to Mother in a low whisper.

Having grown up on a farm, Bertha made frequent references to her animal husbandry skills, so it was a good thing we moved into our own house before Faith was born. Bertha had already made plans to deliver the baby to save our folks the total waste of doctor and hospital money. More accurately, Bertha had made arrangements with Roy to go over and deliver the baby. Roy usually carried out Bertha's big plans. He used to boast, "Bertha's the idea lady, and I'm the make-it-happen man."

Since we'd moved, our visits consisted of their dropping by, unannounced, every three or four months, and our reciprocating to be neighborly and to show appreciation of the past. Even if Mother phoned ahead and gave plenty of notice, saying we'd like to come by on a particular evening, when we arrived, their house always was a catastrophe. Newspapers all over the living room, dinner dishes on the table, days' worth on the kitchen counters. Uncomfortable in such surroundings, Mother would plant herself on the couch with Bertha and not move the whole evening, for fear of what she'd see in the kitchen.

But Roy and Bertha knew their social graces. Roy would tell Dad to "Come on back and let's put the pot on." Dad would try to get into the kitchen first, where he'd snatch up the filthy, greasy aluminum coffeepot and begin washing it out with soap and hot water.

"No trouble," Dad would counter when Roy said not to bother, "I do it all the time at home," which was a lie.

Knowing we were coming, Bertha would have sent Roy to the corner market where he always bought a little square white cake with coconut frosting, wrapped in a cellophane package. Roy would scrounge up six or seven plates or napkins and cut the tiny cake, sometimes foregoing forks if none were clean, and suggest we eat it "picnic style." We kids loved this place:

television, cake, messes, smiles, jokes, and small treats to take home.

Our family arrived at the James' house half an hour early. Roy greeted Dad with his warm handshake and a clap on the back, and ushered us into the living room.

No decorations, I thought. Even Mother puts up some crepe paper at our birthday parties, even if she did re-roll it for the next event.

"Hi, Bertha," Mother sang out as her eyes adjusted from bright sunlight to dark living room. Then the gasp. The newspapers were still there. The dishes were still on the table, but there was a huge teddy bear sitting in the center, like the only remaining sign of life amid the debris following a hurricane.

"Are we too early?" Mother continued, observing the mess?

"Why, no, hon. You're right on time. The kids'll be here in 'bout a half hour. Come on back 'n see what I done planned."

Mother walked into the kitchen. Dirty dishes. No paper cups, no paper plates, no paper napkins, none of the amenities we associated with neighborhood birthday parties. But there were the cakes. Eight small square cakes with coconut frosting, all still in the cellophane packages.

"I've been savin' em up for a slap week now," Bertha invoked. "You know they usually only carry one or two at a time down to Johnnie's." The way I calculated it, there was about half a cake for each guest. What a great party.

"Did ya ever find the candles?" Bertha asked Roy.

"Yeah, I done," he answered as he pulled out a pocketful of half-burned waxy stubs, a variety—everything from used birthday candles to hurricane supplies.

"Well, let's put 'em on," Bertha suggested. "We bought a cake for each year a Kathy Jo Lynn's life. We'll put a candle on each one."

I wasn't exactly a world class hostess or guest, but I knew something was amiss. This didn't look like a Blow Out to me.

Remember Mother's compulsive organization, and remember her teaching background. Before a Blow Out, she would have had lists set up on the backs of the used envelopes to prevent such a last minute disaster. There would have been a list of age-appropriate games and prizes. There would have been a list of supplies to buy or borrow and things to assemble. There would have been a list of things to do, with dates included so that nothing slipped by. There would have been a count-down list for B-Day, H-hour, including every extra task that had to be completed before the guests arrived. And when the guests arrived, the party would have been perfect—not expensive, but perfect.

"Lookee, here," Bertha continued, pulling a dusty 7-Up bottle from under the sink. "We're gonna play spin the bottle. Won't that be cute."

"What happened to the pony rides?" Mother inquired.

"Well, I forgot to call the man 'till this morning. He said the pony has the squirts. Spin the bottle is cuter anyway. I love to see them boys squirm around."

Having heard this twist of events, Joe began begging Dad to let him wait in the car and listen to the radio, but Dad said he had to stay put to be polite. I don't mind saying I was very disappointed that I wouldn't be able to practice the story I'd written titled, "Dale Evans Chases the Seminoles." Dad said galloping a horse through the Everglades swamp would be very wet and very dangerous to the poor animal, but it was my story and I made it go the way I wanted.

Seeing a disaster pending, our personal Superwoman kicked in, and Mother took over. She automatically fell into her crisis-induced Pennsylvania Dutch dialect, which was usually kept under better control. "Do you mind if, to help us, Mercy and Joe, Bertha, pitch in?" she spurted out.

"Well, sure they can, if they wanna. Roy can you find a bottle fer the game? This one has a crack." There are some standards, no matter how low, for something so cute as spin the bottle.

As Joe and I washed some dishes and cleared the table, Faith toddled around the living room, picking up newspapers, and Dad and Roy went out to the shed to find an acceptable bottle.

"Bertha, any paper and crayons or coloring books do you have?" Mother asked.

"Sure, keep 'em on hand for when Kathy Jo Lynn visits," Bertha answered, and then an aside to me, "Yer mama sure do talk funny sometimes."

"A bandana and some clothes pins and an empty jar, I don't suppose you have?" Mother continued. I knew how she operated, and I was proud, knowing she was pulling something together, even if the words were falling apart as they tumbled from her mouth. The minutes were ticking away.

"Give me, Faith, the balloons," Mother commanded. Faith reluctantly handed over the three colorful spheres tied to her wrist. Mack, the filling station attendant had given us one each at the Texaco station on the way to the party, insulting Joe. Mother tied the balloons back together and attached them to the front door.

"Joe, Mercy, stack on the table, next to the teddy bear, the clean plates and forks, and unwrap the cakes and bring in."

Dad and Roy returned with another 7-Up bottle, which had a dead scorpion in it, but by this time, nothing couldn't be rectified. Roy found a stick and poked the dried carcass until the straw-like extremities floated out the end of the bottle with hot water.

There was a quick knock on the front door, and Kathy and her parents, Bobbie Suette and Bubba L., entered. Bubba L. was called Bubba L. to differentiate him from his brother Bubba G. Bubba was a family name passed through Bubba's family. Bobbie Suette and Bubba L. were overwhelmed with the beauty of the occasion and marveled at what the afternoon held in store.

"Oh, me 'n Isabel jus' fixed it up a little. It was nothin'," Bertha assured them demurely, dropping her eyelids, twisting her head to the side a little, and turning an appropriate shade of pink.

When things were as ready for the guests as they were going to get, Mother took a deep breath, and her speech returned to normal, Standard English. "Thank you, *kits*, for your help." she whispered. "You helped make this a nice party for Kathy Jo Lynn."

Soon the guests arrived, and the Blow Out began. Nothing would do but we start with spin the bottle, after all, it is so cute. All eight of us children sat in a circle, even Joe who occasionally glared at Dad, and the bottle spun and wiggled across the floor like a sidewinder ready to inflict great harm. I had to kiss Faith. Kathy Jo Lynn had to kiss the boy with ringworm on his cheek. Joe had to kiss me. I don't remember who the other kids kissed.

Having exhausted herself from the heavy responsibilities of hostess and caterer, Bertha flopped on the couch in her standard check-mark position and watched the events. Not wanting to appear too presumptuous, Mother tried to include her in the activities.

"Do you want the children to play Pin the Tail on the Donkey now, Bertha?" But Bertha was content to watch the impressive events from her lounging vantage point.

Using Mother's quickie homemade version, we finished the game, but not until Faith, who was afraid of the blindfold, had been accused of cheating by the ringworm boy. He yelled, she cried, and Kathy Jo Lynn won. Then Mother realized she had no prizes for game winners, and asked Bertha if there were any.

"No, I jus' thought they'd like money better. Do ya have any dimes?"

Dad found three in his pocket and donated them to disaster relief.

Joe won the game of drop the clothespins in the milk jar, even though I told him he shouldn't have competed with little kids. He said a dime was a dime.

Then we heard a truck pull up out front, and there he was. Flash the Pony. The owner unloaded him and explained Flash seemed better in the afternoon. We were jubilant. Real pony rides. The best party ever.

Wanting very much to take the first ride on Flash, who I immediately renamed Buttermilk so as to make the Dale Evans story more accurate, I slipped over and stood by Roy, put my hand in his, and smiled up as cutely as I could muster. It worked.

Putting my left foot into the stirrup and swinging my right leg, keeping my toes pointed across the pony's back, I professionally mounted my Buttermilk. I arranged the ruffles of my party dress skirt over the saddle and bent over the pony, giving her a nice pat on the neck.

Thank you, Johnny-the-fruit-man at B-Thrifty's, I thought, for letting me spend so much time practicing on your fake pony ride, even if I never had a nickel to put into your cracked ceramic horse. There, there, Buttermilk. There, there, girl, I whispered.

As Flash and I were led around Roy and Bertha's yard

for the second time, in my mind, Buttermilk and I were galloping through the Everglades. I could even hear the splashing of swamp water and feel the moisture on my legs. I tossed my head to the side, flinging my hair into the wind, and as I turned to wave at my admiring audience, I saw a strange expression on Roy's face. When I looked down, it was not swamp water on my leg. Flash's digestive problems had recurred, and we were creating a most noisy and conspicuous pattern on the grass. I quickly dismounted and let another rider take a turn.

After a few minutes of watching the rides, Bertha regained strength, found her Brownie camera, and took pictures of Kathy Jo Lynn on the formerly tan Shetland pony, which now looked as if he wore black chaps on his hind legs.

This was too much. Mother collapsed on the front porch and began laughing. When she regained her breath, she told us this truly was a Blow Out. Pretty risqué for a German princess.

We all loved watching eight-year-old Kathy Jo Lynn puff out all eight candles on all eight cakes as she ran from one side of the table to the other, and Kathy Jo Lynn loved opening her presents. Bertha apologized for not wrapping the teddy bear, and reminded everyone how she'd been far too busy with all of the other birthday preparations.

When the party was over and the children had left, Bertha and Roy thanked Mother and Dad for attending and gave each of us children a nickel for our take-home treat and to compensate for the commandeered balloons. His take of fifteen cents made Joe concede the day had been worth it.

"That was real nice of you to give Bertha a little hand, Isabel," Roy told Mother. "You know she's so busy she sometimes gets behind."

We were sort of stunned as we drove home. We didn't really know what we'd seen. It was the disaster that almost was, but it had turned out okay. Dad reached over and patted Mother's hand. His pride in her was obvious. Faith, Joe, and I deemed it a great party, except for the kissing part, and we kept our manure-covered feet on newspapers, which covered the floor of the car.

My birthday was the next one to arrive. I asked Mother what it would be like, and she said it would not be a Blow Out. I didn't know if she meant a party or a horse.

Chapter 8

"...when the day's work is done,
we go on thinking of losses and gains..."
- Seneca

About the Graces. This time I whispered the words to myself as I lay in bed tracing the outlines of things I thought I saw in the rough sky blue plaster marks on the wall—the head of a dog on the body of a starfish, the profile of a man with a beard, lots of birds, some with three wings. Although I was only eight at the time, as I lay looking at the plaster, I began my own sort of family history, formulated from childish impressions, memorized details, and imagination.

Always beginning with the oldest Grace I could remember, I recited the list of facts, embellished them with my own fantasies, and made the story go like this: Anna Grace had been born to a kindly woman named Maria who had come to America from Germany. Maria had a twin, and their parents lived in a tiny cottage in a small village near York, Pennsylvania. Dad had told me Pennsylvania was just to the right of Ohio. The girls' parents died when they were young, and the twins were taken in by a couple who lived nearby. No one knows much about the family before then.

The girls had similar features, but they were not identical. They had sandy blond hair like mine, and always wore plaits with ribbons, which were like my pigtails, Grandmother said, only much longer. For some reason, no one remembers

49

Maria's twin's name, but I decided it probably was Sophia, the only name I could come up with that rhymed with Maria.

By the time Maria married a man from a nearby German settlement, she was wearing her plaits in wrapped circles over her ears. Note to myself: Learn how to pin my braids up in circles over my ears. That stuck up Sally Sue Van Landingham in my third grade class will be so jealous! I don't think I got over Sally Sue until I had the Taggard twins to fret about in fourth grade.

Great-great-great grandmother Maria began raising her babies, one of whom was Anna Grace, my great-great grandmother. The girls wore dresses down to their ankles all the time and had aprons to wear over them. Mother said they were called pinafores. I hated the sound of their shoes, which were boots with pointy toes. Sounded pretty uncomfortable and unglamorous to me.

Another note to myself: Rearrange my shoes in the closet, this time from beautiful to ugly, and look out for any with pointy toes.

The young lawyer Horace Greely said, "Go west, young men, go west." Anna Grace's husband followed his advice and took the family to Ohio. They settled with their friends and shirttail relatives, although I couldn't quite figure out why a relative would be a shirttail, unless they borrowed your clothes a lot. There, that was it, the first Grace story, a good start. I vowed to pick up the saga again soon, after I arranged my shoes, or maybe the following day.

Tearing into the bottom of our little walk-in closet, I tossed out Faith's toys, my loose paper dolls, and Miss Roberta, my formerly beautiful doll which no longer had legs, thanks to Faith's curiosity about how a doll could be made to walk. Then I found a belt that had fallen and a bug that had accepted tenancy at the Roach Hotel but had not survived to report the amenities.

50

I wasn't the least bit afraid of the creature—you couldn't live in the South very long without either getting used to them or going hysterical like my Aunt Edna did the first time she found one on the kitchen floor in the middle of the night when she went looking for some buttermilk and crackers. Dad and Joe thought her screeching was pretty funny, but Aunt Edna was so scared that she stayed in bed all night from then on.

I'd finished cleaning out the bottom of the closet and began rearranging my shoes very neatly. Cracked patent leather church shoes. Hmmm, heels getting worn down. Chenille slippers. They'd started out shapeless but had developed the shape of my feet, and they matched my robe nicely. Old school shoes for play. Blue leather and beaten up. Hadn't had them on lately since it was still summer. Sandals. Cute but I liked barefoot better. New shoes for school. Penny loafers. A pretty red-brown leather, and Mother had given me two bright dimes with my birth year stamped on them. All the girls were wearing them last year, and I finally got mine, although I did worry about the legality of having dimes in penny loafers, even if pennies didn't fit. It just didn't seem right.

Left shoe. Looked all around for the right one. Back into the corners. Hadn't left it in the closet. Under my bed. Under Faith's bed. Not there. Under the dresser. Not there. I asked the assistance of my family in the search, but no loafer was to be found. Faith was questioned, but being not quite three, she didn't' seem to understand the commotion.

"Well," said Mother as she picked up the roach box to dump its guest into the toilet, "It will show up. It couldn't have gotten far."

A second or two later we heard an "Oh, No!" coming from the bathroom and rushed over to see what was wrong. Mother stood looking a lot like a plumber's version of the Stature of Liberty, holding my shoe with the stick of the toilet plunger. The shoe was dripping wet and curled up like a potato chip. Everyone looked at Faith who grinned a chubby grin and pointed a chubby finger. "Shoe!" she exclaimed, "Shoe!"

The carcass was set out on the back porch to dry, but after a few days, we realized there was no salvaging it. At least I'd keep the dime. I became so consumed with the loss of my right shoe that I took to walking around in just the left one, still admiring it and the brilliant coin. Joe said I was crazy, but if I sort of stood and stuck just one foot out like in the Hokey Pokey, it looked great. If I sat on the couch on the other foot, it looked great.

But great or no, there was just one. I finally approached Mother with the obvious—what was I going to do for school shoes? Instead of going back to the pretty shoe store in Coral Gables, we walked up to Holly's Five and Dime and found a pair of less expensive Mary Janes, a style that NO ONE IN THIRD GRADE WORE TO SCHOOL. I knew it was like having to buy two pairs of school shoes, but I felt new loafers should have come out of Faith's allowance, except she didn't get any allowance.

When we got home, I arranged my shoes again, this time lining up all of my shoes in the closet from ugly to pretty, with the single left loafer making up the end of the row, like an exciting exclamation point following a dull sentence.

Children's minds work in funny ways. I tabled the stories for a while, feeling somehow to blame for my own misfortune, although I could think of nothing I'd done to cause such a detour in my school wardrobe plan. Then it hit me. God was telling me I was pushing too hard for Uncle John information.

Chapter 9

"The supreme happiness in life
Is the conviction that we are loved."
- Victor Hugo

I had this really pretty third grade teacher, but she had an odd reputation and a well-stocked desk full of pencils, notebook paper, erasers, and rulers. She sold them to us students at exorbitant fees when we ran out. To punish one child, she would require the entire class to write all of the numbers from one to two thousand as homework, even though our stubby fingers were nowhere near ready to support such a strenuous and frequent activity. We also noticed and reported home that Miss Lange, who spilled out of the top of her ruffled white peasant blouses, often would yank up her very full skirts and cross her bare, suntanned legs if a certain male teacher entered the classroom, and he entered often. Concerns voiced to the principal by questioning parents seemed to go unheeded.

Note to myself: Get a peasant blouse and wear sandals without socks more often.

"Mercy seems more occupied with entertaining the class than with penmanship," Miss Lange commented on my report card, making my father explode. "That's it. Her penmanship is good for a third grader, and her teacher doesn't even know it." True, I enjoyed making the other kids laugh, but I'd never been reprimanded for it. Taking matters into their own hands, my parents sent me back to Ohio with my visiting aunt and her girlfriend to finish out the school year.

The trip was an adventure I would remember in great detail, and the experience made me feel special and wanted and important. I became close to my aunt and very close to my grandmother, and there were lots of Grace stories.

When asked if I'd like to go to Ohio for three or four months, I agreed quickly. What an adventure, I thought, and what an opportunity to learn more about Uncle John. Go to the scene of the crime. I'd learned that technique on *Perry Mason*.

Mother packed my suitcase with most of my clothes, and I was positioned in the back seat of the car, princess style, with a pillow on one side and a box of books, paper dolls, crayons, and coloring books on the other side. We had barely reached North Miami when I began writing down information and clues that would come in handy when I began my detective work Up North.

The trip north taught me much about the interests of young, single women. One night we stayed in a charming cottage with a wooden glider swing outside where we took the evening air and talked about clothes and shoes and other girlish interests. Note to myself: Ask Mother if I can have mix-and-match outfits to expand the look of my wardrobe, whatever that means.

We drove too late the night before we arrived in Ohio and ended up in a motor court with no redeeming qualities. No charming cottages. No glider. If the Auto Club had rated the sorry structure, it would have been a warning and not a recommendation. We laughed as we squirmed, three in a bed, trying to get comfortable as the rickety place shook with highway traffic from the front and train traffic from the back.

Before bed, we'd crossed the court to the cafe, which was so run down that my aunt suggested we order canned soup we'd seen up on the shelf. After steaming bowls of Campbell's Scotch Broth (don't eat the crackers—they aren't wrapped), we retreated for bed and an early wake up. Aunt Edna had purchased a bottle of Coke from the machine in case anyone needed a drink in the middle of the night—we wouldn't want to drink the water in the room, or heaven forbid, use the glass. Going against strict Pennsylvania Dutch regimen, we forfeited bathing, feeling cleaner not using the facilities. Sort of ice skating along on two hand towels to traverse the room, my aunt carried me from bed to bathroom as the need arose so that I didn't have to get my feet or slippers dirty. We left the dangling light bulb on all night to keep any night visitors at bay, and as we'd settle down and drift off to sleep, either Aunt Edna or her friend Shelly would explode with contagious laughter as she remembered something about our evening's ordeal and attempted to re-tell the tale.

"I thought I had a dark skin rash, but when I got up close, it was only the streak of dirt on the mirror," Aunt Edna said. Then she tried to drift off.

"The hole in the blanket lines up with the hole in the sheet—it's a matched set!" Shelly cried out.

"The waiter fell asleep after he heated the soup."

"There's a box holding up the side of the dresser."

"He said we don't need an alarm clock—the 7:05 rolls through about 6:30 and will blow its whistle."

Laughing is said to be close to crying, and I think we were more hysterical than amused. It was a long night, but we survived and finally reached Niles and the comfort of my grandmother's old-but-impeccable two-story home. Then the real fun began.

My grandmother had not had a little girl to fuss over for many, many years, and she fussed very well. I was living the life of an only child and enjoyed the attention. We washed my baby doll Bonnie Braids and her clothes. Grandma ironed them, even the tiny collar with lace. She bought new patent leather doll shoes from Woolworth's and tied new pink ribbons in her golden hair. Bonnie Braids and I flourished with the nurturing.

My room in Ohio was the one Uncle John had used, but there were no clues as to his disappearance. There were now starched, hand-embroidered pillowcases, beautiful quilts, and even fresh flowers on the dresser. A girl could go to sleep quite happily in this room, but she could not stay asleep in the new surroundings. Somewhere between late night and early morning, I slipped into bed with my grandmother, where I received cuddles on demand and a strong sense of security.

My grandmother spruced up all of my clothes, too. Everything was heavily starched and ironed, and lacking the muggy nature of Miami's weather, they held up until the end of the day. My hair was brushed before bed and brushed and braided in the morning. I enjoyed long bubble baths with as much warm water as I wanted, and I loved every minute.

My days began with a ride in the back seat of Grandmother's car to the school where she taught. There, I joined Mrs. Richard's third grade, and my grandmother went to her own fourth grade classroom. All was not perfect in school in Ohio. It was my first experience with corporal punishment, and I wept quietly as I watched an unruly boy named Denny being paddled as he sobbed and called for his mother. But I liked my new desk and classmates, and yes, even the board-wielding teacher, who did not have to reprimand Denny again for the rest of the year.

The drive to and from school every day allowed plenty of opportunity for lots of talk and lots of stories. Grandmother seemed pleased that I took such an interest in our family's history, and it was during this time that I committed most of the stories to memory, except, of course Uncle John's story. No other relative seemed to elicit such an emotional response, which for the Pennsylvania Dutch means total silence.

My friend Helen lived next door to Grandmother. When I told her my suspicion about Uncle John, she told me just who I should talk to—Miss Little, the librarian at the Niles McKinley Memorial Library.

"Hello, Miss Little," Helen began the first Saturday I was in town. "This is my friend Mercy from Florida. She is doing a school assignment on Nazi spies who live in Niles. Where do you think we should begin looking?"

Miss Little, slightly amused at the request, showed us how to use the huge card catalog and how to find old newspapers for research, but alas, we found no information. Instead, we decided that reading Nancy Drew mysteries would help us learn more tricks for detective work, and we began a contest to see who could read more of them.

The rest of the school year passed in a whirl of activities, most of which I experienced for the first time. I learned how to type on my grandmother's ancient Underwood typewriter. I learned a few tunes on her ancient Baldwin piano. Helen and I took turns ice skating on the slate sidewalk out front of the house in my aunt's ancient ice skates. Who needs ice when slate is available?

Non-stop activities filled my days, nights, and weekends. I rode Old Paint, my aunt's ancient pony at the stable where she kept her fine young mare, Majesty's Image. I went to see every movie approved by Grandmother—Snow White and the Seven Dwarfs, the African Queen, Big Top, and my very favorite, Singing in the Rain. My mother's young cousin Nancy had the record album from the movie, and we sang and danced our way through the music whenever I spent an afternoon at her house.

Grandmother and Aunt Edna took me to the Ringling Brothers Circus and to a seedy carnival when it rolled into town. There I saw my first freak show, including a woman who had a baby growing outside her stomach and a man who swallowed swords. Sometimes we'd go to the city pool, and sometimes we'd walk into town for shopping, including a new pair of penny loafers. Yes, indeed, the life of an only child was mighty appealing.

Most Saturday evenings were spent shampooing, wrapping bobby pin curls, filing nails, preparing for church the next morning. Usually we made a pan of fudge. My mother's young cousins sometimes dropped by, hair already in pin curls, and we'd all wait to see if the chocolate goo would harden into delicious candy. A flock of young and old Pennsylvania Dutch single females on the town on a Saturday night.

We went to the First Presbyterian Church of Niles, where I attended Sunday school in the basement of the same church where most of my relatives had been married and buried. I loved the sense of belonging and history in Ohio.

Behind Grandmother's house stood my great-grandmother's house, where the young cousins now lived. And down the street from it was the grocery store my great-grandfather and grandfather owned. I walked on the wavy wooden floor and imagined how they, too, had walked on the floor and had run the magnificent old cash register. Ca-ching. Ca-ching. In Ohio I had the feeling of a great family, and I felt an important part of it.

Soon school was out, and Grandmother and I boarded a Greyhound bus, heading home to Miami. We carried a *Ladies Home Journal* for her and a *Coronet* magazine for me. As suggested by the old home remedy book, I wore a large piece of cardboard under my shirt to prevent car sickness, which of course, didn't work. We saw much of the countryside I'd seen on the way north just three months earlier and a lot more.

Entering a Greyhound cafeteria, Grandmother would guide me, making sure I didn't touch anything. We sat at the counter so she could watch our cheeseburgers being grilled, and she didn't mind telling the cook to choose a different patty if one looked too dark going onto the grill, or if one looked too light coming off. We spent hours of waiting time in Greyhound stations where the buses assembled and spewed diesel fumes into our breathing space. There were African American people riding up front with us the first day who were moved to the back of the buses and the cafeterias the farther south we went.

Heartily complying with the advice from the bus driver to treat my queasiness by keeping my tummy full of popcorn, I soon was able to enjoy the trip. We read, we watched out the window, and we talked to the ladies in the seats near us. I'd never slept sitting up before and often would awaken to marvel at the tiny lights still glowing over some passengers' seats as they read into the night. I usually awoke in the morning to find myself taking up both Grandmother's seat and mine, with my feet sprawled over her lap. Bus trip or no, we went back to the bathroom and Grandmother wiped down the fixtures using plenty of Lysol from a little bottle. She'd pull our washcloth and hand towel out of her overnight case and begin our routine. I had my sponge bath, my teeth brushed, and my hair braided for the day. I'm not sure anyone who isn't Pennsylvania Dutch can appreciate how important this was for Grandmother's sense of well being.

It was three nights and four days on the bus, which stopped at every hamlet down the Dixie Highway, and then we were on the last stretch into Miami. Although I'd loved my time in Ohio and had enjoyed the life of an only child, I was only eight, and it was time to get back into my own little family again.

I had no way of knowing I'd return north in less than a year.

Chapter 10

"The human language is like a cracked kettle
on which we beat out a tune for a dancing bear . . ."
- Gustave Flaubert

Being a northern transplant into the South, and especially with the Pennsylvania Dutch speech pattern and vocabulary which slipped out now and then, I had the feeling of being an unbiased observer as I noted differences between my family and those we lived among. I heard the rhythm of sentences and the flavor of word choice, and savored the unfamiliar result. Ear candy.

We children picked up a unique way of speaking, made up of a concoction of my father's precise manner blended with my mother's unusual sentence structure and vocabulary, then smothered with a gooey, Down-South topping.

"Hand me from next to you my chooz, please, y'all," was just as likely to come out of my mouth as "Please hand me my shoes, Joe. They're next to you."

Like Mother, Joe and I worked on taming the occasional German dialect, but sometimes it just sallied forth from nowhere. It is estimated there are nearly a million people in the United States who either know Pennsylvania Dutch, or as do many of the Amish, speak it routinely. There were few, however, in Miami, Florida.

Mother said the Southern speech pattern was seductive. Like an artful lover, it establishes itself when you're not looking, especially if you're young. She talked like that sometimes if

61

there was a chance to be poetic. Dad said it was a pretty risqué remark for a school teacher. Mother just rolled her eyes and sighed. He never missed a chance to tease her.

"P'like," Little-Linda-Down-the-Street said to my brother and his friend one day, "Yur th'solgers, 'n me 'n Mercy ur th' nersis." She'd accent the first syllable heavily and drag out the second, making my name sound more like MURRR-See.

P'like is a word heard throughout Southern childhood games, and is a contraction of *play like*. It requires somewhat of a nasal intonation, being best pronounced with the nostrils pulled down and the jaw pulled back, and sounds somewhat like plaque. While most of the English-speaking world gradually adjusted to the new pronunciation of A, E, I, O, and U during the Great Vowel Shift of the 1500s, it didn't seem to take hold for the ancestors of some Southern speakers.

"Win das MAY-re git hom?"

"Lucket thet purdy driss."

"Y'all frum a-HI-a? Am frum Flawda."

We heard our friends asked to be carried to the movies. Instead of merely going to the store, most of them were fixin to go to the store. We learned to say Hey instead of Hi as we passed kids in the hall at school, and we heard multiple names used when we felt one probably was enough. "Hey, Bill Wayne Dudley. Hey, Becky Jones."

Our time in the South gave me the chance to see lives different from ours—to fall in love with some and to disdain others. For the most part, I fell in love. I was the one in the family who saw the variances between our neighbors and us, and I was the one who felt the variances important enough to report back. I'm sure the neighbors were noticing me, too, as I gawked, listened, questioned, snooped, stayed too long, and generally tried to become one of them.

Miss Lily lived down the street with her widowed daughter Martha and her grandson Mikey. I'd never heard anyone in her late sixties called "miss" before, but the sound did roll off the tongue nicely. Since her daughter worked part time in downtown Miami, Miss Lily was generally in charge of the house and the boy, and she provided my first glimpse into classic Southern gentility. Born in Georgia in the 1880s, and the granddaughter of a Civil War captain, Miss Lily was still in love with the Confederacy, but she didn't hold it against me that I was from Ohio—how could a child possibly be responsible for making the choice to be born to Yankees?

"Cum awn en, dorlin'," she'd drawl when I peered through the front screen door like a bold Peeping Tom. Sometimes I had to wait for her to answer the door, and I'd bend down to handle the bleeding hearts blooms growing in the merciful shade by the stoop.

"Are Joey or Mikey here?" I'd ask, pretending to look for my brother and her grandson.

"Ah think they wen' fishun' up ta the canal, but y'all come awn in 'n all fix us some iss wotter."

Once in the small two-bedroom house, I began a trip that could have happened in Savannah or Atlanta as easily as in Miami. Like Miss Lily, herself, everything in the house was diminutive and elegant and antique. The living room had a pie crust pedestal table to hold the little television, and the dining room had a drop-leaf table and four upholstered chairs artfully arranged next to it, making a crescent shape. Most of the house looked like a dark museum, except the Florida Room, which had lots of light and a large grass mat that smelled like the air before it rains. This was the room where Mikey kept his toys and where Miss Lily sewed. All-in-all, it was a comfortable home which was impeccable at any time of the day or night. With a once-a-week housekeeper, Miss Lily never appeared untidy nor seemed to have housework to catch up on. Years later in my own home, when no one else was around, I'd seek the coolness of my living room on summer afternoons and sit among our nicer things and regain that feeling of tranquility I was introduced to so many years before.

Although most of the ladies in Miami did not wear nylon stockings in the summer, Miss Lily did, even with her daily house dress and white wedgie sandals. On Wednesday afternoons when Martha got home from work, Miss Lily would be outfitted in a nice dress and would have the card table ready for the weekly canasta party. My mother usually attended these evening gatherings, so I had a natural excuse to crash the events, even though I was routinely warned not to drop by except for an emergency. But I had to see who wore what, if butter cream cake was being served, and if the nuts this week were my favorite cashews. Miss Lily would greet me with, "Murcy, darlin', we were expectin' y'all. Come awn en."

"Mom," I'd begin earnestly as Miss Lily led me to the dining room to make contact with my mother, "Dad wants Faith to wear her long pajamas to bed. Isn't it too hot for them?" There. Sincere concern. Hmm...Mrs. Shipley has on her wooden Cuban sandals and her hair is pinned up on top her head in curls. Mrs. Peterson has coral nail polish and looks really tan tonight. Mother looks nice in the mint green lawn dress we'd finished up just this afternoon—I'd handed her the fifteen little buttons she'd sewn down the front. Martha Jensen wore what she'd worn to work—a summer suit my mother called it—and low white pumps.

After accepting just a few nuts and mints and a disapproving look from Mother, I scooted home with the news that the long pajamas would be all right for Faith—it wasn't supposed to be really, really hot. Later, in bed, I'd go over every lovely detail of the party that I could remember: They used the Haviland candy dish, and the fingertip towel in the bathroom was the one I'd ironed when Miss Lily had let me help. Beautiful images to inspire beautiful dreams.

Other nights I'd report that the kitten hadn't come home for dinner or that Joe said he was going to listen to Red Skelton on the radio, and I was afraid of stories about skeletons. Sometimes I'd show up just in time for dessert, and Miss Lily and Martha would assure my mother that I was very welcome to join the ladies. Later, I would escort Mother home and hold the little trinket she'd won if she'd done well at cards that night.

When I was really young, I couldn't understand why my mother said Miss Lily was pretty. I knew I liked her, and I knew she wasn't ugly, but I didn't associate pretty with old women—to me pretty was reserved for the young and for movie stars, and of course, Miss Florida, but only until someone was thirty. Then it was all over. Eventually I saw the curly silver hair which was styled every week at the beauty shop in back of Mrs. England's house. I saw Miss Lily's rosy lipstick and her face made up with loose powder and clouds of rosy rouge, which created a soft look like a warm sugar cookie. Yes, I finally realized, Miss Lily was pretty, and she was becoming my fantasy grandmother, my Down South grandmother, good until the real thing arrived on vacations.

My nearly daily visits allowed me to watch Miss Lily stitch linens and hem skirts, to look at pictures in her photo albums, to watch her chop fruit that Martha bought at the docks from the huge boats coming in from the Caribbean. I was allowed to dig into her cedar chest and try on her wedding dress and the Confederate captain's jacket, which had been wrapped in tissue paper and stored in an old, broken-down cardboard box. "Ya know there, dorlen', we didn't git any gran dottors," she'd begin, "N I'd jus like ta 'dawpt y'all." We both knew she wasn't serious, but I appreciated the approval.

So it came as a shock when Martha hinted that Miss Lily was beginning to sip the sherry too much and to forget things. Martha called it "goin' 'rown the bend a bit." Mother remembered how Miss Lily was drinking three rum and Cokes during canasta while the other ladies nursed one all evening. Dad, who'd walked up to their house to replace some plumbing, remembered finding several bottles of liquor in the dark, dank cupboard under the sink, way in the back like hiding hoodlums.

Coming to Miss Lily's defense, I assured my parents she kept one bottle of rum and one bottle of sherry way out in the open in the cupboard, next to the Cheerios. But Joe remembered playing in their Florida room one morning and seeing Miss Lily napping on the living room couch. Mikey was concerned because she always slept from one-thirty to two-thirty, and always on top of her neatly made bed in the bedroom. When they checked on her, they smelled alcohol and phoned Martha, who came home from work. By then Miss Lily was up and fixing lunch for everyone.

From that point on, Miss Lily was a magnification of herself. Her hugs were tighter, the stories of her girlhood more detailed, the naps longer. Everything was Miss Lily squared.

The Wednesday evening canasta parties became an embarrassment for Martha. Her mother would smile her wide smile, showing the Roses are Red lipstick smeared across her teeth. One time, as Miss Lily slipped into the kitchen to refresh the drinks with new ice cubes and Coke, Mother noticed one of her rolled nylons had gathered at her ankle like a beige silken bandage. She forgot the nuts for the party and insisted, against Martha's wishes, on sending me to B-Thrifty's when I dropped by on my regular reconnaissance mission. The other ladies, in best Southern fashion, pretended not to notice. But, oh, how they talked the next day.

"Was you-know-who tipsy again last night?" Mrs. Shipley telephoned my mother.

"I just don't know what's going on with her," Mother tactfully replied.

"Well," Mrs. Shipley continued, "Sondra Peterson thinks she's hittin' the bottle pretty regular, and I think it's just plain awful! Why doesn't Martha do somethin' about it?"

"Let's hope she'll be better soon. I gotta run. Bye now."

For me, this was the time when my visits brought forth the best of Miss Lily's stories—how she was the first girl in her town to go to college, how she met her husband Peter, how her grandfather felt about Peter. And on and on and on. Soon I became the expert on Miss Lily's life, stunning even her daughter with occasional comments about relatives she, herself, had long forgotten. Like my own ancestors, they were real to me, not just dead people. They moved with all the beauty and courage of movie heroes and heroines without any of the contamination of the realities of life. It was as if I was helping Miss Lily paint a picture of her past and her family for the ages. Our version became the official version, just by sheer repetition.

And then, for some inexplicable reason, Miss Lily put her rum and Coke down one Wednesday evening and announced that she didn't think it agreed with her anymore, that it made her too dizzy nowadays. And with that single act, the morning naps and the afternoon stories came to a halt, and we just picked up where we'd left off many weeks previously, with less fervent need to delve into the core of her memories. The facts had been stated, embellished upon, cleaned up nicely, and taken their place in history.

Chapter 11

*"May God grant you many years to live,
For sure He must be knowing,
The earth has angels all too few,
And Heaven is overflowing."*
- Irish Blessing

"Out, out, Spam dot!" Christopher Joseph Malone, my father, called out at breakfast one morning, having just flipped a greasy slab of the canned meat onto his shirt. He wasn't able to resist the opportunity to mix corn with Bard. That is how my father lived. The humor was always simmering near the surface like a teakettle, ready to boil into a whistling stream of double meanings, puns, or the incongruity of life.

"Did you ever notice," he once observed, "that Mr. Black is a white man, that Mrs. Christiansen is Jewish, and Sandy Watters hates the beach?" Of course we hadn't noticed, and we laughed at the connections, all true. Joe and I tried to bring even greater incongruities home for his approval, but Dad was the master.

Although he expounded on the oddities of life, Dad didn't talk much about his family when we were little, and it seemed as if I had to pick out threads of information one at a time before I could weave a picture of his early years. But once he began a story, it was long and intricate and told in the Irish way with lots of description and wit.

Dad seemed to know everything. He was my encyclopedia-on-demand, and if he didn't know the answers to my questions, he knew where to find them. And it was not all serious information. He felt no pun too corny, no play with words too absurd. "You'd better order a Six-Up," he whispered to Joe one day. "We're too poor for the higher version." He loved a good audience, and we always loved opportunities to crack up, as it was called in those days.

Born at home in Ohio on Christmas Day, 1914, my father was the youngest of ten surviving children. They were called Lace Curtain Irish—defined as having a fruit bowl on the table and, of course, lace curtains in the windows. He had just enough English blood to provide a love of Shakespeare, Chaucer, puns, and Yorkshire pudding.

The basic image I've put together of my father's early life included parochial school in a cold climate with strict nuns teaching uniformed children. Saturday afternoon confession and Sunday morning mass. Although my father described Sunday mass as a wonderful event full of ritual, music, and the beauty of the church itself, his whole religion-centered early life sounded rather somber and routine to me, but Sunday mass was followed by Sunday dinner. That's where the fun seemed to start. It was a huge event, served in two sittings to accommodate the fully assembled family, which usually included the families of married daughters. The children ate at second table, and the beef-stuffed adults, relaxing nearby and squirting tears of emotion and laughter, repeated tales of the early life in America and the old life in Ireland. Thus the family stories were passed down generation to generation.

"Ahhh, Little Chrisssstopher, eeeeat your green beeeeeans. You know we didn't have much fooood when we came to Amereeerica, and your graaaaandfather here can tell you about being a chiiiiild in Iiiiireland during the Great Faaaamine. They gave the poooor little chilldren green badaaaadas to eat so they'd get siiiick and not want fooood and not cryyyy from hunnnnger. Now eeeat your green beeeeans."

Well, that's a cheery topic for Sunday dinner, I thought. And even though he wouldn't admit it, I imagine my father stillll didn't eat his green beeeeans.

There was no variation in the menu. Roast beef, mounds of mashed baDAdas, a green or yellow vegetable that my father would not eat, bread, and the favorite Yorkshire pudding. It's not a dessert. Yorkshire pudding is made with one egg, one cup of salted flour, and one cup of milk, mixed and baked in a scalding cast iron skillet which has been oiled with beef drippings. It is then drown in gravy. Although my own mother often served a leg of lamb or a ham at our Sunday dinners, my father's preference for the beef-potatoes-pudding soon made it our favorite, too. Dad's favorite dinner became our standard Sunday fare. Yorkshire pudding in Miami was about as common as cheese grits and catfish in New York, but once our friends tried it, they smiled up at Mother just like one of the family when she asked who wanted the last piece, even though we knew it always went to Dad. It meant so much to him.

Not the typical Irish with red hair and blue eyes and freckles like Arthur Godfrey or Mickey Rooney, my father's family were Black Irish, thanks to the Spanish Armada. As the ships wrecked in storms off the coast of Ireland in the 1500s, some of the sailors invaded my father's homeland, and I guess invaded some of the women who lived there, too. The mix gave my Irish ancestors the dark hair and dark eyes, and skin that tended to burn in the sun but then settled into a nice, deep shade of mahogany tan. When we learned the Spanish Armada part of our family story, Joe liked to say his real name was Jose De la Malone and wouldn't answer to anything else for a whole week that summer.

My father's family had broad smiles and noses, a

generally conservative outward demeanor, but always with the pixie ready to surface at any opportunity, some more appropriate than others. Like Dad's conference with my Latin teacher. Afterwards, she was forever telling me to give my father her best and to tell him, "Artis longus. Vita brevis," which I gathered was a joke about some man named Arthur Longbottom who died at the age of twenty. I didn't see anything particularly funny about it, but Dad would laugh out loud and say you had to have been there.

Being the baby of the family, my father was cherished and spoiled by his older sisters who dragged him around like a baby doll of their own. He preferred tagging behind his older brothers and became a good athlete and mechanic by watching them, but his greatest love was literature. Books, books, always books. When we were growing up, there were scattered Shakespearean references like, "Rough winds do shake the darling buds of May," when a hurricane was approaching, or when school was starting in the fall, "Summer's lease hath all too short a date." It was natural, it was perpetually present, and it was Dad. Think about my parents—a man who loved the English language, and a woman who routinely mangled it.

It was difficult sending children to Catholic school during the poverty of the 1930s, but the results made it a bargain. At high school graduation, my father knew he wanted to earn the first college degree in the family, and he wanted Notre Dame University, the capstone education for a Catholic male. At Notre Dame he waited on tables in a fraternity house and worked on a liberal arts degree of science, history, and literature. The summers were for earning money and relaxing,

Although Mother had a different take on the story, according to Dad, they met during the Great Depression—it was the summer between his junior and senior years at Notre Dame University in Indiana, and she had just graduated from

Kent State Normal School, the two-year teachers college in Ohio. Dad liked to tease and tell anyone within earshot and a few beyond it that some people had to go to college to learn to be normal. Mother usually responded with a glare and a sigh.

The Depression and the cut back at the steel mills around Youngstown forced some of my father's married sisters to return to their parents' home with their expanding families, leaving little room for Dad. He joined some college friends at Lake Milton and lived in a cabin that sounded only a little better than Uncle Tom's, but, of course, it was Up North, and there was no Simon Legree, unless you consider my stout little German grandmother who, with the help of a broom, protected her daughter from that black-haired, dark-skinned Irishman who was probably an Italian or a South American if the truth be known. Black Irish, indeed.

My father and his roommates played catch on the narrow dirt road which joined Dad's cottage and Mother's, and when he saw her come out of her house on a regular basis, looking cute in her shorts, he purposely began throwing the baseball into her yard. Then she'd have to pick it up and give it back. He said she'd bat her eyes at him when she handed him the ball and say, "Here's your little ole baseball, honey," which I knew was a lie because she never talked like that. Incidentally, I tried batting my eyes, but couldn't get the hang of it. Joe said I just looked like I needed glasses.

Dad said he took one look at Mother and was gobsmacked, an Irish term for thunderstruck, by her beauty and intelligence. My parents began talking and going down to the beach to swim in the chilly waters of Craig Beach, but as they swam and danced under pavilion lights, and their romance developed, they knew there was a huge problem: religion. Very few Catholics married out of their faith in those days, and very few Protestants converted to the Catholic lifestyle. My mother also faced the dilemma of not being able to teach if she married. That was the standard then. Teachers couldn't be married if they were young, and they certainly couldn't wear shorts in public or go to night clubs or wear much makeup or do anything that sounded remotely like a little fun.

Thus, when fall approached, my father went back to Notre Dame, and my mother went back to her first classroom, but they saw each other once or twice a month and wrote frequently. There was no engagement ring or other outward sign to raise questions. Finally, one Saturday night when my father was home from college, and without notifying anyone, my mother slipped into her blue satin suit. She and my father drove her new Packard to Pennsylvania and were married by a justice of the peace. No priest or minister to deal with. No relatives to appease.

Then it was summer—my father had graduated Summa Cum Laude and had landed his first professional position, and my mother had fulfilled her school contract. They shared their secret, were feted by friends, and awaited both the birth of my brother and the beginning of World War II. They went their separate ways on Sunday mornings.

When Joe was born, he was baptized a Catholic, but the issue remained unresolved for many years. Suddenly, we were of Sunday school age— I'd been running around for six years without being baptized and was at constant risk of eternal damnation, plus we had the new baby's soul to consider. So my very Catholic father and very Presbyterian mother put their differences aside for the sake of their children and compromised on becoming Episcopalians.

Anthropologists often divide families into extended and nuclear categories. Nuclear families rely on themselves. They are usually seen in industrial areas—families who have moved away from the clan for employment opportunities or advancements. Each unit functions in its own small group—no relatives to please, no relatives to accommodate, no compromises needed.

Extended families are usually found in agricultural areas. Many relatives to rely on to bring in the crop or to handle the animals. Many relatives to please, many relatives to accommodate, many compromises made.

My family had made the swing from extended to nuclear status with the move to Miami, and although there were no close-by relatives for my parents to appease, the break from their churches was still a very difficult decision, especially for my father, who never really reconciled the change, and in the end was buried in the Catholic church with a Latin service and the appropriate number of nuns to help guide his Irish soul to heaven. And to be a good audience.

Chapter 12

"Every miller has a golden thumb."
- Geoffrey Chaucer

"Sorry, Mr. Malone," Dr. Procter told my father, "this didn't heal up like it should have. I'm gonna have to give you a skin graft."

"Well, where will you get the skin?" my father asked.

"I'll take it from your hip. I won't need much. You'll only have a small scar." Dr. Procter assured him.

At the time, my father was teaching English and French over at South High, and being left-handed, he managed to pull the paper cutter arm down, severing both the Tuesday vocabulary quiz strips and the top of his left thumb, which the school secretary Miss Mitchell later found when she cleaned up the mess. Not knowing what to do with it, she stuck the chunk of skin on the bottom shelf in the ice box of the office Kelvinator refrigerator, just in case it might come in handy later. It was that kind of innovative behavior that had gotten her promoted up from mimeograph operator.

The principal, Mr. Mahoney, whom the students, of course, called Mr. Baloney, sent my father directly to Dr. Proctor, who used a series of large, fluffy, clumsy knots to stop the gushing wound. Dr. Proctor liked to tie fly fishing hooks, and the thumb less resembled a medical procedure than a Wormy Jim with Feathers, which everyone knows attracts trout.

Back in the classroom, Mr. Baloney, who was liked by neither students nor faculty, tried to explain both the blood on all the words from *judicious* to *mercenary* on the Tuesday vocabulary quiz and the students' missing teacher, but within the hour, the rumor had circulated that Dad had both been fired and wounded by the dangerous principal.

My father got back to Room 16 about 1 o'clock, and he and his thumb enjoyed being a novelty throughout the school. By 3 o'clock, votes and bets were being taken on naming the fly fishhook thumb, and at Friday's assembly, J. William Burkeston from Mrs. Cavenaugh's tenth grade homeroom won four dollars and fifteen cents on Maloney's Baloney for Abalone, a clever combination of both my father's and the principal's names. Most of the students didn't care that abalone was a shellfish which would never open its clammy mouth for a worm with feathers.

After two weeks, Maloney's Baloney for Abalone still wasn't healed up or trying very hard to, which is when Dr. Proctor told my father about the skin graft from hip to thumb.

"Well, you know I have hair on my hip, Doc. What will happen to the hair?" Dad whispered to Dr. Proctor since Nurse Ada Lynn was within ear shot in the exam room.

"We really aren't sure, are we?" Dr. Proctor answered. He did know my father was pretty hairy, having previously complimented him on the luxuriant curls on the tops of his toes at his school physical.

"By the way," Dr. Proctor continued, "I hear the students over at High have named your thumb."

My father chuckled, "Yes, they call it Maloney's Baloney for Abalone since you like to tie fly fishhooks. I added abalone to last week's vocabulary quiz.

"Well, you get on out of your pants now, and let's get goin' on the graft," Dr. Proctor said as he grabbed up a pair of scissors.

"Uh, Doc, aren't grafts usually done in the hospital by

plastic surgeons?" Dad asked.

"Well, sure, if you wanna go that route, but it's just a quick little deal, and we can be done in 'bout twenty minutes."

"Okay, let's just get it over with," Dad decided as Dr. Proctor began removing the stitches from Maloney's Baloney. Dad soon found himself draped in a green cotton nightgown and lying on his right side where he could study the small red rose pattern on the peeling wallpaper, rather than face Ada Lynn, who was actually quite pretty, even with that eye that sometimes went off to the side, and you didn't know which one to look at.

Dr. Proctor grabbed a dusty old book titled *Elementary Surgery* and used a full bottle of 7-Up to keep it open at the "Grafting, Hip-to-Digit" section. He whipped out a large hypodermic needle filled with an anesthetic from behind his back and stuck a spot on my father's left hip, just below the birthmark that's a remarkable likeness of the State of Texas, if you don't mind the panhandle being on the wrong side.

"Now pour some 7-Up into the paper cup, Ada Lynn. That'll keep this skin strip alive while I stitch up his hip," Dr. Proctor commanded. Dad was finally told to turn over onto his back and to put his left hand on a towel. The thumb was soon repaired, this time with seven stitches and knots, and it looked like a monk with hair all the way around the bald spot on top, except it wasn't completely bald because, like I said, my father had that hip hair. Incidentally, my father never drank a 7-Up after that day.

The thumb was not bandaged because Dr. Proctor thought it was better to keep it out in the air where it could heal, but he did give Dad some salve which slicked down the hair and knots like Brylcreme does.

Dad rushed back to school so that he wouldn't miss the cafeteria lunch and have to settle for a wrapped salami sandwich and a Nehi orange from the Winn-Dixie like he did after the first doctor visit. This was fortunate since it was Wednesday, hamburber-gravy-over-mashed-potatoes-with-corn-and-red-cherry-Jell-O day at school.

Dad's class was intrigued with the new look of the thumb, and once again votes and bets were taken on the best fly fishhook name for it, and once again, J. William Burkston from Mrs. Cavenaugh's tenth grade homeroom won with Thumb from Bum for Catching Chum. He wisely added an explanation to his entry, reminding the students of what some people in England call a rump and what some people out West call bait. Mrs. Cavenaugh made a mental note to talk with the school counselor to see if J. William wouldn't be a good candidate for a scholarship to Florida State's Writing Department.

The purse, which was awarded at Friday's assembly, was ten dollars and seventy-five cents. J. William was later heard to say he hoped Mr. Malone would get hurt more often because this extra money was coming in handy, and he'd sure like to get a car when he turned sixteen.

Six weeks later, the thumb was completely healed. Dr. Proctor bragged that the key was keeping the skin strip in 7-Up during surgery.

Miss Mitchell, the school secretary, found the original thumb tip when she defrosted the Kelvinator in June before summer vacation started and gave it back to my father. She thought he'd like to keep it like she'd kept her gallstones.

By then, J. William Burkeston realized there was little hope for more accident money to increase his car fund, and got himself a job at Ernie's Shell Station over by the Monkey Jungle.

Unfortunately, the hip hair continued to grow, and being a southpaw, Dad never did get the hang of trimming it with his awkward right hand, and had to have it trimmed every two weeks when he went to Bob's Bait and Barber for his regular haircut. Bob didn't charge for the thumb, but Dad always added an extra nickel to the tip for his trouble.

Chapter 13

"Go clickety-clack, O pony hoofs
along the street."
- Carol Sandburg

Dear Gramma,

How are you? I am fine. We had an avacado fite in Mr. Castle's orchard. Otis-the-Egg-Man saw us and chased us out. Joe got red marks where he was hit. He had to take a bath. Then we got his bow and arrows and tried to shoot the tree. Mikey shot Joe by mistake. There was blood on his leg. Not like at the movies. Real blood. I ran home and told Mother. Joe had to take a bath. Two in one day. Mikey didn't tell Miss

Lily. I did and Mikey got punished for not being careful. He can't play outside all weekend. Now Mikey is mad at me. Miss Lily says he will get over it. Mother put the bow and arrows away. She said we can't play with them for a while. Then I had to take a bath and Faith had to take her bath. She splashed so much water that Mother laughed and had to wipe the floor. Then Mother took her bath. She made a meat loaf for dinner. Daddy ate it a lot and I like it very much. Faith hid hers under her plate. Joe found them and ate for her. Does Uncle John like meat loaf? We have been taking swim lessons at the Venetian swim pool. It is big and pretty. It has caves and trees. Faith has to watch. There are no swim lessons for little kids. My bathing suit crawls up and I do not like it. Joe is teaching me Canasta and we play. Faith wants the cards. We give her old ones and she likes it. How is Aunt Edna? How is her horse? I want to see it. Can she ride it to Miami when she visits? I still have my cow girl suit but it is short. I put it on Faith. She likes it. I am tired.

Love, Mercy. XXX OOO   I love you. I miss you.

P.S. I am having a birthday in 3 weeks and what do you want to get me. Then school starts. I have Miss Hume and Joe has Miss Lord and Faith has no one. Mother teaches her. You can get me anything I like. Tell Aunt Edna my birthday is 3 weeks and a new cow girl suit is good. Uncle John can get me anything too.

Chapter 14

"He that loves a rosy cheek...."
- Thomas Carew

When we were eleven and nine respectively, Joe began training to become an acolyte for the priest, and I began rehearsals for St. Cecilia's Girls Choir. This was a period in our life when we became totally settled in the St. Philip's Church family. Helping us singers dress some Sunday mornings, my mother was a choir mother, and helping gather the tithes, my father was an usher. Even Faith Rose—who was now a member of the preschool day school—went to the nursery willingly, if not enthusiastically.

I looked forward to the Thursday afternoon choir rehearsals. Going straight to church from school, there was even time to get sick on the swings in the park across the street before practice. During practice we girls would sing softly or loudly under the direction of Mr. Andrews, who accompanied us on a grand piano. He had a deformed index finger, which he waved enthusiastically and frequently like a pirate's hook, adding an element of interest and fear to the sessions.

Mavis, an anemic type girl, usually slouched over in her chair and mumbled the words. This would annoy Mr. Andrews, who would remind us, without singling out anyone, that we were to "Raise voices in praise." Being the very obedient type in those days, I threw my tiny chest out farther and farther, and sang out louder and louder. No one told me I was generally way off key. We knew practice was over when Mr. Andrews would begin banging out, "This is MY country, land that I LOVE!" Topping this upbeat ending with cookies and punch, we were filled with the spirit.

Then it was my first Sunday to sing. Being the shortest member of the choir, I walked in first with my next-shortest-member partner. We were preceded by the crucifer and his cross, and were usually followed by the priest. Father John Carroll, our very proper rector, terrified me since I'd seen him tug on an older girl's newly pierced ear and earring and tell her to take the earrings off—it was not proper to be decorated while in choir garb with anything but a cross. The girl cried, her ear bled, and she ran upstairs, leaving her partner to enter solo.

Part of the intimidation I felt from Father Carroll also stemmed from a choir dinner party I'd recently attended and where Father Carroll had reigned. We four youngest members had sat at a card table together, trying to remember our best manners, but as little girls often do, we began the uncontrollable giggling. It all began when Mavis whispered the secret, "Carroll is a girl's name." To nine year olds, this was a hoot. Like hyenas at a tea party, we giggled, saw mashed potatoes in Mavis' mouth, giggled harder, and marveled at her impressive entertainment. Too good to hoard, we passed the secret to the next table, where it landed like an unexploded bomb.

Father Carroll tried to be friendly that evening, and he wanted to know what was so funny. Mavis confessed the awful truth. Father Carroll looked shocked that we'd dare such a comment and that we'd actually admit to it. We spent the rest of the miserable evening smothering the aftershocks of laughter, wondering how we could have been so familiar with such a holy man, and comparing the punishments we expected to await us at home.

The following Sunday, Father Carroll did not enter behind the choir, but was waiting in the wings to make a less spectacular entry. It must have been the one-Sunday-a-month communion for the family service. Whatever the cause, I knew he was watching as we bowed at the altar, turned, and entered the choir section, and I was scared. I was also the owner of large facial cheeks. One of my father's nicknames for me was Fattos Cheekos, which was usually followed by a big kiss on the apparently irresistible, ample mounds. Evidently Father Carroll thought I was purposely puffing out my cheeks because, still in hiding behind the partition, he puffed out his cheeks and stared at me.

Oh, no, I thought, "He's still mad about the Carroll thing. Or maybe, like earrings, large cheeks are not suitable for a pious look."

Never being one to react to crisis sanely, and trying to face a tense situation with humor, I puffed my cheeks back at him, Louis Armstrong style. Father Carroll's eyes grew large. He jerked his head back, regained composure, looked away from me, and quickly entered the church.

That's it, I thought. I'm going to hell and I'm taking these huge cheeks with me.

Chapter 15

"Though they go mad they shall be sane. . .
And death shall have no dominion."
- Dylan Thomas

"Hey, Joe, why do Mom 'n Gramma 'n Aunt Edna all have different stories about where Uncle John is?" I challenged my brother as he stood at his workbench, gluing together some pieces of a model plane and whistling the tune to "Up in the Air, Junior Birdmen." This was the Air Scouts' favorite song, and Joe hoped to join when he was old enough. Usually Joe wouldn't get into family stuff—he didn't seem very interested in that sort of thing. But that day, it must have been the Duco cement fumes, he became more verbose.

"Wha da ya mean?" he mumbled.

"Well," I continued as I fiddled with some of the gizmos on the workbench, "Mom says Uncle John lives with a cousin in Ohio. Aunt Edna says he works out of state. Gramma won't say anything. Didn't you know that?"

"No. Don't mess with those model pieces. I need all of 'em. Didja ask Mom what was right?"

"Ya, but she doesn't talk about it. She won't say anything. Just like Gramma. Nobody says anything."

"Usually, when you get so many stories," Joe continued, "it means none of them are right. Remember *Perry Mason* when that lady told the police she'd been at her daughter's house the night her husband was murdered? But she'd already told her neighbor she'd been on a little vacation. Hamilton Burger had her arrested because her stories didn't match. Perry knew there was a different story. The real story."

Wow, he could put things in a way I could understand—pure television. Note to myself: Watch more *Perry Mason* and watch it more carefully.

I flopped on Joe's bed, traced the outlines of the maroon dogs, and recited the next installment of the Grace stories. Despite his protestation of being too busy, I noticed he stopped gluing sometimes and listened. Although I didn't understand all the grown up terminology in the story I'd memorized, it went something like this:

Anna Grace grew up in Ohio and married Charles when she was young, and they had a little girl named Caroline Grace who was our great-grandmother. Caroline Grace had many brothers and sisters and grew up in a comfortable setting. They attended the First Presbyterian Church where my great-grandmother met William, who would become our great-grandfather. Earlier in his life, William had worked in the local nail factory, were he caught the tuberculosis that would kill him many years later.

The local newspaper chronicled their engagement and marriage, describing Caroline Grace and William as "a popular young couple." Note to myself: Become popular at church.

Great-grandma wore her hair twisted on top of her head, and the pictures show heavy beaded winter dresses and white summer dresses with tucks and lace. Grandma called them frocks. Note to myself: Get a summer frock. If I couldn't know those other Graces, I'd at least know their trappings.

Great-grandmother Caroline Grace led a social life, a combination of church, ladies aide, family, and friends. She had my grandmother Margaret Grace just before the turn of the century....

Joe dropped the Duco cement and interrupted, "Okay, Mercy, knock off the story. I wanna go swimming." Apparently my fascinating recitation of the Grace saga had lost its appeal.

"And don't bug Mom about Uncle John," he added. "I'll find out everything for you."

Chapter 16

"Of all those arts in which the wise excel,
Nature's chief masterpiece is writing well."
- Sheffield, Duke of Buckinghamshire

January 2, 1953

Dear Happy Homemaker at Miami Gazette,

Since you want helpful hints to print in the paper I have some for you. I have saved them up so you can choose which ones you like best. Here they are. I will send more later.

Bertha James

IRONING. You don't have to iron if you have your husband pick your landry off the line real careful. Take 2 baskets out and toss everthing you don't want pressed in one. Have him to fold everthing you want pressed in the other. Then in 2-3 days everthing at the bottom of the basket is ready to wear. The shirts look particularly professional since they has fold lines in them.

SCRUBBIN YOUR FLOOR. When they say on the radio that a cane is a comin' be sure to sprinkle Tide all over your floors. Porches too. Then when it's time to mop up after the cane passes over your floors is clean. Even the carpets but some suds may work up for a month or two. Some years is better than others for canes and clean floors.

DISHES. If someone real snooty is a comin over put your dirty dishes in the oven to hide them. But don't forget like I did and a week later heated the oven for a TV dinner and have all your plastic dishes melt since it is a big mess for your husband to clean up.

CUTTIN YOUR OWN HAIR. I don't like to pay good money for a shop cut so I made up this way you'll probably like it too. Just wrap your hair in bobby pin curls as usual and then take one out at a time and snip an inch or so off. This works real good except like when Wanda up the street got called out to the front stoop and forgot to finish cutting and later wrapped her hair back up and had one side of her head longer than the other at church the next morning but she shoulda wore a hat and not blamed me. P.S. Wanda I am ready to make up if you are.

CUTTIN YOUR HUSBANDS HAIR. Is a lot like cutting your own hair but he gets real mad if I tell anyone I put him in bobby pins so just keep it to yerself. Just pin his top hair in curls and trim as usual about 2" on the top and 1" on the bottom. Next row is with scissors. Also I use my carrot scraper on the neck because I like to cook my carrots with the skin just scrubbed and not peeled away. A little salt and butter is good over them or for a fancy dinner like for Jeff Davis Day, you can add pepper and chop a onion to spice it up real nice.

BABYSITTING. How to keep a baby happy. Put him on newspapers in the corner of the kitchen. Give him a big piece of bread with lots of jam. Don't clean him up when hes done. Give him a feather to play with. He will try to pick it off one hand and then the other for a long time. Clean him up good before his mama gets there.

Happy Homemaker at newspaper, this is all for now but I have more and will send them in when I have more time to write.

Chapter 17

"Spread me all over vit busser
and cham a piece of bread."
- From the Pennsylvania Dutch

Mother came from a long line of Kauffmans and Kramers. German-Americans were conservative, stern, and clean. They cherished their kits (kids), but knew where to draw the line. No childish brux or grex (pout or complaint) went unnoticed by parents or Deutch Uncles. German is the only language which has a word like *schadenfreude*, the good feeling we can get when something bad happens to someone we don't like. It is honest, and it is hard. But the way of life also maintains lasty (long) relationships and produces stability--few nix nooks (hell raisers) among them. Mother says the closest they usually get to swearing is *cripes* or *crimeny*, but I could mention a few times when she's gone way beyond that.

The Pennsylvania Dutch are frugal. I didn't say cheap. Cheap means you always try to get someone else to pay for things. Frugal means you figure out ways so that no one has to pay much for anything. Although my mother's people had a little money, they taught their children and grandchildren that there was no excuse to waste. It was standard practice for my mother to punch out only one or two of the holes in a can of Bab-O so no one would squander a wasteful full shake of the cleanser. We turned collars and let down hems. We took mayonnaise jars of ice water to the drive-in movie, and when we were really little, Mother sewed play clothes for us from colorful feed sacks which had come from my grandfather's store, a mere thirty years earlier. As I grew older, my skirts and dresses often were made from lengths of fabric that had been in Mother's cedar chest for decades, and a remnant of material from a skirt or a blouse would show up as a contrast piece such as a collar or pocket or sash on another home-sewn item. Finally, the smallest scraps were worked into patchwork quilts. If I put several articles of my clothing on one of the big quilts, it would have been hard to tell where my wardrobe began and where the quilt ended.

The Pennsylvania Dutch women had closets of expensive china and trunks of beautiful linens which were to be saved for "good," an elusive state, which meant they seldom got used and usually were passed down to yet another generation. When I went to college, I needed a blanket for my dorm room, and my Aunt Edna offered a gorgeous blue wool one from her linen closet. The blanket was in its original crackly cellophane wrapping, and the style of the label indicated it was approaching heirloom status. As I opened the package and shook the blanket out, I sneezed and spit as it disintegrated into shreds of wool and strips of shiny satin binding. The blanket had not made it to "good."

Nothing slips by the Pennsylvania Dutch money watch. Not even my grandmother's prize-winning pumpkin pie escaped economy. Grandmother refused to sell her recipe to Mr. Baker for Baker's Bakery, but she fiddled with it to save a penny or two on her own. The recipe calls for two eggs, and on the old scrap of brown paper, my grandmother wrote, "I use one for economy." This verhoodles me (bewilders me). Grandmother wouldn't divulge the recipe for mere money, but she'd risk a runnier version to save the cost of one egg.

I can imagine her reaching up to the newspaper-lined middle shelf of her pantry and pulling out the light green mixing bowl she'd won at a showing of *The Best Years of Our Lives* at the McKinley Movie Palace on Wednesday Dish Night. I can see her pushing the light button on as she went down cellar to retrieve the eggs, walking across the cold, wavy cement floor, pulling the egg bowl from the cooler, debating on how many to use, and then lifting out just one. I can imagine her climbing the rickety wooden stairs back up and feeling just a little smug at her decision. The funny thing is, using only one egg never seemed to have made a difference. The pie was always perfect. Grandmother, of course, never splurged on whipping cream for a topping like the extravagant Italians across the street did.

Frugality, however, could never interfere with cleanliness. Clothes may be inexpensive, home-made, patched, and pieced, but they must never be dirty. Clorox was always purchased by the gallon, although it was rumored the larger-sized jug may actually make one more reckless and wasteful.

Cleaning house goes beyond the regular redding up, and it was our Saturday morning ritual. It often wrecked plans with school friends, but it was always first priority. Dad laughed at Mother's cleaning. He said the Irish "keep the pig in the parlor—the pig is Irish, too." He made it sound more like "Irish stew," which Mother pointed out was why she cleaned every Saturday and redded up morning and night.

Mother was as beautiful as Elizabeth Taylor, with black hair and blue eyes, but very little makeup. She gave me so many gifts over my lifetime, and I think the greatest gift was her curiosity. It was urgent and uninhibited and complete, and it was not uncommon for her to read an article and then explode with enthusiasm about some obscure fact—like when she read about seahorses.

"Joe, Mercy, did you know that the male seahorse carries the young?" Mother said one day as she collapsed the newspaper into her lap. All of us were startled. Mother generally avoided any discussion about something as personal as a pregnancy, even if the pregnancy was for a lowly seahorse. Dad was surprised, too, but it was his scientific mind that reacted, not his sense of propriety. He said that a male seahorse carrying the young was an impossibility. By the very definition of male and female, the phenomenon would make the male the female and vice versa. Sort of a scientific typographical transposition. No matter, Mother was excited and went to the encyclopedias to continue her search. After documenting the news article as accurate, she set up a trip to the Miami Seaquarium, where she questioned experts in more detail and tried to see some pregnant males up close, and Dad grumbled and went to watch the sharks.

Thinking back on my mother's ancestors, there really was more to the Graces' lives than just cleaning—they loved teaching. Not wanting to make out (stop) the tradition, and being women to go to (to be naturally inclined to) teaching, my great-grandmother taught school before she got married, my grandmother taught school when my grandfather died and my mother taught school from the age of 20, taking time off to launch her kits (kids). Teaching reinforced the disciplined lifestyle, since a good classroom was a well-controlled classroom.

Mother grew up in a mixed neighborhood, and without even knowing it, took on some of the more carefree attitudes of her Italian, Polish, and French neighbors. Then she married an Irishman, shocked the family, and edged into an even more relaxed lifestyle. But the roots of the Pennsylvania Dutch were still there. For breakfast, we had cold cereal, a gooey version of French toast called ekk bread, fried slabs of cold mush, oatmeal, or dippy ekks, over easy to the general population. "Lift from the pan a dippy ekk," Mother would sing out some mornings. Then we would dunk our toast into the soft yolk—a dippy egg, descriptive and yummy.

However, when a girl is in junior high school and is dressed up after church in a dress pretty enough to wear on

Bandstand, and is with her friends at the Happy Hen Breakfast Shoppe and can't find her favorite meal on the menu, and she asks if they have dippy ekks, and her brother looks horrified and her friends laugh, and the taunts produce an achey belly and there's no appetite left, and afterward her father tells her it is no big deal, and her mother gasps at what she has caused, then the girl finally demands the proper terminology for egg dishes. Over easy. Over easy. Over easy. They say if you repeat something three times, it will be yours for life.

By the way, that particular afternoon I, I mean "the girl," pulled down the Pennsylvania Dutch cookbook and buried her sorrows in a pan of futch.

* * * * * * * * * * * *

FUTCH

From Mrs. Jacob Billig
Mercer Township

Make the pan reddy – schmutz up vit oleo.
1 pawnd or mar pawdert shocker
2 cup coco pawder or mar
1 pawnd marcharin or busser – make melt all
over
Wanitta – vun shot
Salt – throw pinch uff
Mix me up – schmutz in pan
Needs sefral ares fer cool
Check to see harten the goo.

* * * * * * * * * * * *

Chapter 18

"...waiting for a gift from the sea."
- Anne Morrow Lindbergh

Summer days and nights in Miami are muggy, so to escape the heat, we used to make frequent trips to all of the nearby beaches. We played in the ocean, ate our picnic lunches in the breeze, and walked up and down the shore, looking for shells. Sometimes Dad gave us a nickel, and we'd run to the snack stand for ice cream cones, chocolate, of course.

Because my parents were really good swimmers and divers, they missed the water during the week. Dad said cool-offs and evening dips and weekend entertaining in our own swimming pool sounded really good. He got up early one Saturday morning, saluted us and said, "I shall return." Mother said that General McArthur said the same thing when he left the Philippines. Dad took the pick ax and shovel from the garage and began digging. Mother was so afraid of sidewalk supervisors and neighborhood gossip that she swore us to secrecy. Dad said it was unnecessary and that the Manhattan Project was less guarded.

"Just don't say anything," Mother began. "He may change his mind or find out it can't be done. And then we'll look silly." Since there were no fences or large shrubs to hide him and the hole, it was difficult for Dad to keep the secret very long. Finally the bomb dropped, and, yes, we had sidewalk supervisors, and, yes, we were the topic of neighborhood discussion. But soon enough the neighborhood was more interested in Amy-Next-Door's new boyfriend who took her walking into the avocado orchard at night.

To protect neighborhood children and other trespassers from danger, Dad had to build a cement block wall around half of the back yard, since the pool hole was legally considered an attractive nuisance. You guessed it. Joe began calling me that, too, except he said the attractive part may have been a stretch.

As my father worked on the wall, he measured, mortared, lifted, and tamped, and I rode the empty wheelbarrow back to the piles of dry cement, gravel, and sand on the far side of the yard. We soon developed a little ritual so that I would not miss out on homework time. Dad would lay my spelling list for the weekly tests and for the BIG school spelling bee on the wall, hold it down with a block, and call out the words, over and over and over. After weeks and weeks of drill, I was ready for the BIG spelling bee, and, like Mrs. Fisher's parrot, could recite most of the words for fourth graders accurately and on the first try.

My father, however, was also my downfall. He had some funny Up North sayings, which he recited with a forced heavy accent. One of his favorites was "Hit's over there, behint the chair, with hits overhalls on." He explained what overhalls were—work clothes for men. Although I picked up on the fact that Hit's meant it is, I had no reason to know that he had been purposefully and playfully mispronouncing overalls.

The morning of the BIG spelling bee was very warm. I awoke early and with a good case of the jitters.

"Mom," I began, "can I wear the pink skirt you put rick rack on?"

"Sure," Mother agreed, "and I'll iron and trim your pink ribbons so they look better."

The skirt had been let down to accommodate an unusual growth spurt on my part, and the new white rick rack camouflaged the hemline mark.

"Let's see, Mercy, wear some white socks. I polished your white sandals last night when I was up with Faith."

Mother took extra care with my hair that morning. She took the ancient curling iron, the one her mother had used on her, and laid it on the electric stove burner to heat.

"I'm going to make two pony tails and curl your bangs," she told me. "Hop up in the high chair, and let's get going."

I sat up straight in Faith's high chair, Mother's kitchen beauty station, and she began brushing vigorously and quickly.

"Ouch, they're too tight, Mom," I complained when she finally finished putting my hair into two bushy pony tails secured with green rubber bands from the *Miami Herald*.

"Oh, they'll loosen up, Mercy. This way they'll stay nice all day."

"They're pulling my eyes tight," I complained, "I look Oriental."

"Do you want to look nice up on stage? I wish I could be there to see you, but Faith's really sick with tonsillitis. I was up with her off and on all night. Hold still, now. Let me do your bangs."

Mother pulled the hot curling iron off the stove and through my bangs, twisting them into tiny ringlets.

"I smell feathers burning. Do you smell feathers burning?" I asked.

"No, it's just some dry ends of hair. Hold still now so I don't burn your forehead."

That kept me still and quiet.

The BIG spelling bee was held about nine in the morning, and all of the school gathered in the auditorium, where three fourth graders from each class, including that stuck up Sally Sue Van Landingham, went up on stage. The principal called out word after word, and student after student had to sit down. On tiptoes and sputtering into the microphone like a buzz saw, I took my turns, which included words I remembered from my list—*Mississippi, submarine, February, enough, famine.*

Between turns, I was nervous. I sat on my chair and swung my feet back and forth like duck paddles, making the tips of my sandals barely drag on the dusty stage floor and turning the toes of my socks a grey-brown color. I fiddled with the hem of my skirt and admired the new rick-rack, and managed to turn the neat meeting of the ends into a frayed, fuzzy effect. I'd also been flinging one ponytail around, still trying to loosen it, but only causing the ribbon to come loose. None of the contortions I performed resulted in a tied bow.

Despite my declining appearance, and as Joe later reported, very distracting behavior, the BIG spelling bee progressed. Soon only one other third grader and I were left on stage. It had come down to the spelling bee—down to Sally Sue Van Landingham and me. To finish before the bell, the principal went to a list of words that we had not studied. My next word was *overalls.*

Well, I thought, I've pretty well won this spelling bee. Won't everyone be proud! I stepped up on my tiptoes, grasped the microphone pole for balance, and carefully spelled the word that I'd heard for years and years. "O - V - E - R - H - A - L - L - S." Smiling broadly, I waved at Joe in the audience, and beamed up at the principal. Ignoring me, Mr. Doyal turned to my opponent, Sally Sue Van Landingham, and asked her to spell *overalls.*

Why would he do that? I wondered. Why does she have the same word I had? Why is my teacher motioning me to sit with my class in the audience? Then it hit me. Mr. Doyal thinks I misspelled the word. I was bewildered at how his list could have been misprinted, and how he hadn't caught the error. Should I say something? It was fear rather than gentility which prevented my blurting out my concerns. Again, I looked at Joe, who was also motioning me to come sit in the audience, and I retreated like, as he later reported, the runner up in a two-girl beauty contest.

That night, laughing all the while, Dad begged my forgiveness, promised to try to keep his Ohio witticisms under better check, and invited me out to the pool project to listen to our new portable radio. I made another note to myself: Stay away from men in overalls.

On radio evenings, I lugged the huge RCA Victor box outside and tuned in to the happy music coming up from Cuba. When Dad requested, I'd change the station to hear the news in English. In order not to waste batteries, my father turned the radio off when he provided impromptu civics lessons and political commentaries. It was, however, awkward when the local news gave updates on the police investigation of a downtown massage parlor and its activities. I didn't understand what the big fuss was over a Swedish massage, not that I knew what a Swedish massage was, but it seemed to make Dad snap off the radio and quickly begin another topic as he muffled out the trail of words and static.

Although there were many spectators during the pool project, there were no helpers. It was my father's baby. He conceived the idea, and he provided the labor. And his face lit up one Saturday morning about a year after the project began as he tied a rag around the fire hose nozzle to protect the delicate plaster, turned the faucet on high, brought water up from the well he'd hand drilled, lifted Faith and me into the shallow end, and watched as we splashed in the puddle forming in the deep end.

We applauded as the water level rose and rose. Dad bowed deeply, and instead of passing out cigars like he did when Faith was born, he invited everyone to jump in and cool off. But we just kept clapping. We were acknowledging every task he'd performed, from planning, digging, drilling, blasting, hauling, lifting, plastering, and painting. We continued clapping for every sacrifice he'd made, from budgeting, scrounging, giving up golf, developing bursitis in his left shoulder, and tolerating all of the suggestions and comments.

It didn't matter the pool wasn't heated. It didn't matter we had to drain it and hand scrub it for a year before the filter project was completed. We love it and lived in it. Our swimming improved, as did our social lives. We soon had legions of new friends from miles around who would show up afternoons or Saturdays in swimsuits and ask if we could play.

The pool was the neighborhood novelty. There were many in nearby wealthy Coral Gables, but none on our side of Red Road, and my parents shared it with anyone and everyone who did not sport a communicable lesion.

The pool was the best part of our house, my favorite part, even if it was built by a man who was sometimes known to wear overhalls.

Chapter 19

*"Some people expend tremendous energy
Merely to be normal."*
- Albert Camus

"They're having a Tom Thumb!" I yelled, slamming
through the screen door one day when I was in third grade. I'd
run home from the bus stop to spread the good news. "They're
gonna have another Tom Thumb, and I get to be a bridesmaid!"
Mother smiled at my good fortune, even though she knew it
meant work and money on her part.

Tom Thumbs were more accurately Tom Thumb
weddings, pageants of tiny bridal parties and ceremonies, but
everyone in the South knew them by their first names.

Just think, a Tom Thumb! In the past, like the majority
of the school, I'd only been chosen to be a guest, and I felt
my chances of being in the wedding party were pretty well over
since the roles were usually reserved for the younger children.
But this year, due more I'm sure to my shortness than to my
acting ability, I'd been included. From the moment my teacher
announced the roles, I'd begun dreaming of the floating froth
of lace and net I'd become.

"Who's the bride?" Mother asked.

"Little-Linda-Down-the-Street," I replied.

At first Mother seemed surprised. I knew she felt Little
Linda was rather plain, but then she responded, "That's no
wonder. They give so much money to the PTA."

Ignoring the note of acerbity in Mother's voice, I

111

corrected her. "No it's a reward for good classroom behavior. They told us that at school. There are going to be twelve of us in the wedding party. And a minister."

"Oh, well," Mother sighed, "Did they tell you what you should wear? Will your church dress do?"

"Oh, they said we could use our mothers' dresses if we wanted, just so it's a pastel color. Do you have a pastel bridesmaid dress?"

"Heavens no, Mercy. We didn't have fancy weddings when I was growing up. We were in the Depression."

I knew what that meant—the Great Depression lecture. Three dresses. One for church, one for school, one for play. Then rotate the good one down as the old one wore out. Use the old one for spare pieces for the sewing basket. And homemade Christmas presents and nothing on your birthday and being cold to save the coal and walking to school in the blizzard to save gasoline and money, and....

"I know, Mother, but what will I wear?" I easily made the transition from her troubling past to my brilliant future.

"I don't know, Mercy, I'll think of something." But I did worry. I WOULD NOT WEAR MY CHURCH DRESS. This was a wedding, and I was third most important, behind the bride and maid of honor. No matter the groom—he was some boy I didn't know, and the boys just wore their church suits and didn't look any different anyway.

"When is the Tom Thumb?" Mother asked.

"It's Friday night, December 15. The last day of school before vacation."

"Well, that's two weeks away. We have plenty of time."

"They want a report on our outfits next week. Maybe we could go up to Holly's Five and Dime and get some material and a pattern," I suggested.

"Well, I guess I could take the dress apart later and use

112

it for something else," Mother considered. "Or maybe there's something in the cedar chest we could use." Her practicality and ingenuity were kicking in.

A trip into the cedar chest was an aromatic adventure among aging treasures. The chest was huge, more like a trunk, covered with a criss-crossed pattern of maple-colored veneer, and it held my mother's satin wedding suit, her diary, letters from my father, souvenirs from the 1939 World's Fair and other ties with her past. It also held the practical—linens, feed sacks, and lengths of yardage. Nowhere near as exciting as Miss Lily's cedar chest. No wedding dress, no veil, no captain's pistol, or so I thought. We children were unaware of the old gun well hidden under stacks of hand-embroidered dresser scarves, tablecloths, napkins, and pillow slips.

Mother took the yardage out. It wouldn't work—plaids and fruit generally were not considered bridesmaid fabric. However, underneath was exactly what we needed. Lace curtains. Stacks of lace window curtains—leftovers from my father's home after his parents died. Mother was a fan of Margaret Mitchell and *Gone with the Wind*, and by golly, if Scarlett could make an outfit from window coverings, so could she. As we pieced and pinned and made a plan which involved flowers from an old Easter hat, I became more and more enchanted with the potential gown and with the thought of creating something from nothing. The genes of frugality were well planted in my nine-year-old brain.

"Time to start getting dinner ready, Mercy. We'll work after supper on it again," Mother said in her Pennsylvania Dutch way. Excusing myself from the cooking, I made my way to Little-Linda-Down-the-Street's house to tell her the good news.

"Little Linda," I gushed, "my mother's gonna make my bridesmaid dress out of beautiful curtains, and we'll pin. . ."

"Curtains!" she exploded. "For God's sake, MURseeee,

y'all can't be wearin' curtains! I'm wearing' Momma's weddin'
dress 'n veil. She's cuttin' it down just for me. You gotta git
yerself somethin' respectable." Quite a mouthful for a first-
grader, I thought, and she gets to say God.

Having been treated as an adult since birth, Little
Linda was more socially aware than I, even though she was two
years younger, and a bit more of a brat, if that was possible. She
called her father by his first name, Tyler, and bossed her parents
around like she did their dark-skinned maid.

"Momma!" she wailed, "MURseeee's gonna wear
curtains to the Tom Thumb! I'll be the laughing stock of Sunset
Elementary. I can't have my bridesmaids wearin' curtains! Call
her momma right now and git this fixed!"

Stunned, I waited for her momma's response.

"Now, don't be ugly, Linda," her momma replied. "I'm
sure Miz Malone's makin' somethin' looovely for MURseeee."

But Linda was adamant. "I can't be getting' married
with curtains in my weddin'! Call her momma right now!"

So she did. And I ran home.

Mother was on the phone when I came crashing
through the door for a second time that day.

"Well, we're not really sure what we'll make, Elaine, but
tell Linda not to worry. Mercy will look just fine. Bye now."
Click.

And then with bewilderment in her voice, she turned
to me, "Cripes. What in the world did you tell them, Mercy?
Do they think I'd use red-checkered gingham or something? I
can't believe the nerve. . ."

"For God's sake, Mother. . ." I started to reply, Little-
Linda style, and then caught myself.

"Mercedes Grace Malone," Mother shrieked, "You are
NOT to take the Lord's name in vain! You know that. Just wait
'till your father gets home." I was definitely getting tired of

being yelled at on this day that was supposed to be so filled with beauty and frills.

I started again, "I don't know, Mother, I just said we were using curtains for my dress and Little Linda got so upset."

Mother calmed down, and somehow we got through dinner, although my father, brother, and I had to endure the entire story, several times. And I had to repeat the Ten Commandments, several times.

After two or three evenings of cutting and basting and pinning, we had the start of a gown, which actually was quite lovely. Then it hit me. It wasn't pastel. I made the mistake of telling Little Linda that it was white.

"Only the bride wears white, for God's sake, MURseee!" she wailed. "I'm the bride. You're not the bride. You can't be wearin' white!"

Again, a pathetic report to her momma, who again reminded Little Linda not to act ugly, and who again phoned my mother to remind her that only brides wore white. I got a better head start running home.

"Well, we're pinning some crushed velvet purple roses at the neck and waist, Elaine. We'll be adding color. Bye now." Click. "That's it, Mercy. I told you not to talk to Linda about the dress. If any more I hear about it, I'll call the school and tell them you can't be in the silly Tom Thumb. Who dreamed this up anyway? We never in Ohio heard of them." There she goes again with the backward talk, I thought. It's going to be another fun dinner.

Finally it was report day at school. Each girl in the wedding party described the outfit she would be wearing. I specifically didn't mention curtains, but I did say it was white with crushed velvet purple roses at the neck and waist. Little Linda gasped but said nothing. She didn't have to say anything. The wedding director told me the dress couldn't be white. Get something else. End of discussion.

I was afraid to face Mother that day, but Joe said I couldn't hide in the shade of the huge hibiscus bushes any longer, and dragged me through the front door.

"Mom," he called out, "Mercy's dress can't be white." Simple. Clean. I was afraid of what Mother was going to say, but she'd already been thinking about the problem.

"Come on, Mercy. Joe can watch Faith. We're walking to Holly's Five and Dime to get some Rit color dye. We'll dye this dress and be done with it all."

The woman's a genius, I thought, as we headed back up to Bird Road. Mother had Grandmother's habit of sometimes kicking a stone when she was walking great distances—it was some sort of diversion to make the walk shorter. Today's kicks were long and hard and accurate, and I stayed in the hindmost position.

The next day when I got home from school, there was the dress. Dyed a pale lavender and pinned with the crushed velvet roses, it was a dream and was exactly what a proper Pennsylvania Dutch girl who didn't use the name of the Lord in vain would wear to a wedding.

The night of the Tom Thumb finally came. Mother, Dad, Joe, and Faith dressed up, and I floated around the house feeling much too pretty for mere mortals. I'd been allowed to wear a pair of Mother's nylon stockings safety pinned to my underpants, and a pair of her low, white pumps. Mother pinned my braids up over my head and secured them with another small bouquet of crushed roses, making a small floral headpiece. She kissed me and said I looked good enough to eat. Dad commented that he wanted me always to be a bridesmaid and never a bride for a long, long time. Joe said I'd have no choice. His own awkward gesture of sibling support. Faith held onto my dress, rubbing it between her little fingers over and

116

over and over.

At school the wedding party gathered behind the auditorium curtains to assemble the procession. The director handed out small bouquets to the other bridesmaid and me. Beverly's dress was light pink and together we made a nice picture. The director handed another bouquet to Little Linda, who, even at six years old and dressed in frilly attire, looked like a spinster. Thick glasses with pointed frames, wispy black hair, thin face and pointed nose. But she was a bride, and she played it for all it was worth.

"MURseee and BEVerleee, come straighten my train, y'all...Is my groom here yet? Make my flower girl stop throwin' her petals around'...Fix my veil, y'all. I swear, I have to look after everythin' myself...Were those really curtains, MURseee?" Her way of offering a meager compliment on my most beautiful dress. "Dontcha jus' LOVE my satin pumps, girls? Momma found 'em for me at one of those darlin' little shoe shops over by Burdine's. Go signal my daddy to come on back and make my picture."

It was then Tyler Cunningham, proud father of plain Little-Linda-Down-the-Street, arrived with his expensive camera gear to photograph his princess. The flashbulbs popped blue and flew out of the camera over and over like baseballs out of a batting machine. As Tyler made Little Linda's pictures, she posed and smiled and generally conducted herself as would have a most disagreeable grown-up bride on her wedding day. Beverly and I stayed out of the way.

When we heard the music, the director motioned us to prepare for our entrance, and Tyler returned to his seat to wallow in the wonderfulness of the evening. I'd heard he'd even planned a reception at their house for anyone who cared to drop by. I could pretty well guarantee my mother would not attend.

"Here... comes... the... briiiiide. All... dressed... in whiiiite." the guests in the audience droned as Beverly and I made our way down the aisle.

Everything went well with the procession--Beverly and I wobbled and clomped in our mother's high heels and felt magnificent. The flower girl still had a few petals to sprinkle, and the ring bearer stood with the groom like a man of consequence, although his hand-me-down jacket had rolled sleeves and hung to his knees like a circus clown.

Then Little Linda appeared. She smiled the radiant smile of a Miss America, and the rhinestones in her glasses picked up the light of the auditorium, making a kaleidoscope of sparkle and lace. Little Linda looked as lovely as she could, and when I glanced at her parents, I saw tears rolling down Tyler's grinning face. My own family beamed but retained their composure, except Faith who called out, "Mercy is so pretty tonight," making me smile demurely in deference to her most valid observation.

The ceremony was a success, if there are criteria for judging a Tom Thumb. Maybe the fact that no boy pushed or shoved and no girl tripped or fell. The giggling was kept to a minimum, and the PTA was able to take up an extra large collection. Tyler Cunningham dug deeply into his pocket that evening and declared loudly that it would be a lot less noisy in the auditorium if every father put folding money into the tray instead of change. The PTA president loved him.

When we got home, Joe and I ran down to Little Linda's to sample the refreshments. We were duly impressed at the lights and activity coming from the Cunningham's tiny home, which never looked quite so festive, even during their yearly Christmas extravaganzas. In the living room, twisted crepe paper streamers made a huge white X from corner to corner.

As the muggy night progressed, the X drooped lower

and lower until it caught Mrs. Cunningham's feathered hat as she walked through the room. Joe snickered and received disapproving looks from the grownups.

The dining room was set with a lace tablecloth, a silver punch bowl, nut and mint trays, and a huge wedding cake, which was an exact duplicate of the senior Cunningham's own wedding cake. Little Linda circulated a photograph to prove the point. They included the small, traditional southern chocolate groom's cake, but the groom, having voiced his displeasure at having to participate in the Tom Thumb and having to let Little Linda kiss him at the end of the ceremony, was heard to say that there was no way in Hades that he'd go to a reception, too. He was currently sitting in his house in his jammies, tolerating his brother's jeers and trying to erase the memory of the evening from his mind.

Tyler stood in for him. He and Little Linda toasted one another with a special punch they said was right out of the prestigious River Road Cookbook, and circulated a copy which was dog-eared at Trader's Punch, rum added for grownups.

Little Linda and Tyler posed for pictures and cut the cake with Little Linda's small white hand resting gracefully on Tyler's large red mitt. Because she wanted to dry her real bouquet, Little Linda tossed a substitute bouquet, a few closed hibiscus blooms tied with a wilted ribbon, and her mother caught it. There was something odd and symbolic about the event, and Joe and I were tiring of the tragedy.

I'd accepted as many compliments on Mother's lace creation as I needed, so I agreed when Joe said it was time to go home. We thanked the bedraggled and hatless Mrs. Cunningham, who still held the pitiful flowers and still held back the tears. It was dark out and we ran home to report on the event and to empty Joe's pockets, which contained additional stashes of candy and nuts.

That night, as I fell asleep with a fistful of mints in my mouth and a troubling vision of the Tom Thumb in my brain, I wondered what my own wedding would be like. Maybe Mother could use a tablecloth, and....

It was good that Little-Linda-Down-the-Street and her father had their moment of glory, since the following week, and most appropriately in the toy department of Burdine's, selecting yet another Christmas gift for his beloved daughter, Tyler Cunningham dropped dead of a heart attack. I imagine he took the image of his wedding girl to the grave, and I imagine the image is still giving him pleasure today—long after Little Linda grew up to become a most gracious and beautiful bride, a real bride. Tyler's younger brother escorted Little Linda down the aisle at her wedding, which was only slightly less spectacular than the Tom Thumb of so many years ago.

Chapter 20

"...and shutting her in with greediness,
The Heavens that do push their bolt against so many."
- Petrarch

Dear Dear Gramma,

How are you? I am fine. How do you like
my new handwriting? I am making curls on it to
be fancy. We had a Tom Thumb at school last night
and I got to be the bridesmaid. Mother made me
a dress from curtains. It is pretty. We will save it
for a Halloween costume now, but we may need the
curtains for the bathroom window. Then it won't
be a costume. It will be back a curtain. Mother said
you didn't have wedding dresses. Just suits. You
will like my dress when you see it. If it is hanging
on the bathroom window I can still tell you what
it is like because I have it memorized. Will Aunt

Edna have a wedding dress or suit? Little Linda down the street was bride. She had a party. We got nuts and cake and mints. I looked beautiful. Do you know Christmas is coming? We have sent you and Aunt Edna and Uncle John presents but I can't tell you what. Do you like sweaters and a hanky? Does Aunt Edna like a fancy hair brush and comb and mirror? Does Uncle John like shirts and fudge? When will your package get here? I will watch the mailman for it. When will you visit next summer? I love you so much and have been a good girl all year in case it makes a difference when you shop and send.

Love and kisses,

Your first grandgirl Mercy Malone

P.S. I won't use this handwriting again. It is too hard.

P.S.S. Does Uncle John have fancy handwriting?

Chapter 21

"Much may be said on both sides."
- Joseph Addison

Dear Editor of Miami Gazette,

I was mity distressed to see your article on them kids what want the govment to help them finish college. What in the world does them kids thank? That were made a money? Us taxpayers alreddy pay way too much taxes. Them kids should just git out and work more. When I was a girl me and sis got the Sears catalog and seen the purtyst driss you ever seen. It had a white colar and ruffles down the front and I don't remember what color it was becos the catalogue was in them brown colors they use to use. We was purty near the same size so we could share it. It woulda been our shinin pride and one or other would look good at church ever other week. We asked our mama if we could have it for three dollars and she said heck no gals we don't have that money. Now git on out or I knock the tar outa ya. Well me and sis said wed work for it and mama said OK you can have one penny for ever hunderd flies you catch in a cannin jar. Mama was real particular about germs. Well we knew jus wear we could git plenty flies and that was down to the pig pen but I think mama realy wanted them from the house. Well me and sis would take the canning jar and begin a chasin flies. We had to wait til after chores to start this job but we got a good jar full but when we counted em it was only 3 cents worth or 3 hunderd and some flies but by then mama had got 2 dresses from Aunt Theola Thurlow what she had saved from when she didn't weigh 300 plus pounds. Me and sis loved them dresses and bought Aunt Theola 3 cents worth a hard candy and she apreciated it. So college kids should jus git out like me and sis did and make their own success altho there aren't many flies down here in Miami like they was up at the farm and anyways mamas been dead since the 1930s. By the way I like to discuss politics as you can see from this here letter.

Bertha James

Chapter 22

"Nothing so fortifies a friendship as a belief
on the part of one friend that he is superior to the other."
- Honore de Balzac

There weren't any girls really close to my age in the neighborhood for many years. Little-Linda-Down-the-Street was only four when we moved in, so I was lucky Joe considered me his friend. I was his acolyte, standing aside, admiring everything he said and did, and imitating as much as I could handle.

If I was Joe's most frequent room guest, his next most frequent guest was Miss Lily's Mikey LeRoy, who was between Joe and me in age. We were a blond-haired, blue-eyed trio, and ran barefoot together in the summer and rode the school bus together every winter. Actually, Mikey LeRoy and I ran barefoot. Joe was prone to athlete's foot and was forced to wear sandals and white socks. The only time he didn't seem to mind this humiliation was when Mikey LeRoy or I came hobbling home with a row of grass stickers firmly implanted in a sore foot.

I realized the two boys were really friendly rivals, rather than best friends. They were different in many ways. When Joe rushed into his room dripping wet from the pool, seeking either sympathy or medical assistance, he unconsciously fell into Pennsylvania Dutch dialect and informed us, "I've been bitten through the trunks by a bee." An unimpressed Mikey said he would have just said, "Ouch!"

It was barely seven or eight feet diagonally from my room

to Joe's, but the distance was only measurable by considering the social span. By going to Joe's room, I could leave the immaturity of babies and baby toys and enter the world where my intellect had to be stretched to keep up, and where there was a friendly person willing to share his knowledge. I don't think Joe realized the great and positive influence he was having on my childhood.

Joe and I both liked to read, and coinciding with our increasing reading levels as we grew older was a set of World Book Encyclopedias, a gift from our grandmother. This was no junior edition. It was the real thing. The books were kept in an oak cupboard near the entrance to Joe's bedroom door, and he gained his knowledge easily, I think through osmosis as he slept at night. I gained mine by sheer numbers of hours spent with the books. This was my newest and greatest fascination. When I opened a heavy maroon volume, the glossy paper was cold to the touch. Every page had facts. I was not a methodical reader like Joe. I did not start on page one of Volume A and read straight through. I was a browser. I learned how a volcano was formed, and I saw the change in each letter of the alphabet from ancient to modern times. I read and read and read. I knew Truth was at hand, and it was manageable.

Joe's room became the official clubhouse, and the club depended on his current interest. I tagged along for everything from Cub Scouts to Air Scouts. We knew our roles well: Joe was the general—he provided the stuff, be it equipment or idea. Mikey was the sergeant—he supported ideas and contributed muscle. I was the buck private—I did whatever they said.

The room also was the scene of debate and analysis. These discussions reflected our juvenile perceptions, such as thinking they could do anything on TV as we endured Mikey's theory of how the tightrope walker on the *Sealtest Big Top* jumped rope on the high wire. It involved something about scotch tape and string and ended with Mikey's being invited to go home.

We were not afraid to debate more serious matters, too, as we did the day in 1956 when we saw a picture in the *Miami Herald* of a B-26 bomber, which had crashed into a neighborhood in New York. Postulated: We need to help if a plane crashes out on 58th Avenue. Resolved: I would be sent out to rescue passengers. Mikey would take the garden hose from the side of the house and put out the fire. Joe, the owner of several Erector Sets, would lay claim to the wreckage and begin salvaging parts. Note to myself: Read that First Aid pamphlet again.

When I was about nine, the boys sent away for stationery which had been advertised on *Space Patrol*, their favorite television program. This naturally led to a Space Patrol club, and I was very pleased when they told me I was the secretary. My duties? Make Joe's bed and clean the clubhouse. My rewards? Since I'd contributed twenty-five cents toward the cost of the stationery, I could handle it but not write on it. This seemed adequate to me. A quick tug of the maroon or ivory dogs, and I could marvel at the sheets of sky-blue paper with rocket emblems, the matching envelopes, and even the stickers which would announce our Space Patrol membership on the boys' notebooks and other valuable documents. Life was rich, indeed.

Joe received a small printing press for Christmas one year and established our three-person newspaper production, located, of course, in his bedroom., Our jobs were explicit: I gathered the news, wrote the news, and printed the news. Sometimes I was allowed a few turns of the press arm, and the little sheets of paper would fly out, wet with ink and wonderfully pungent. I was in charge of selling subscriptions, and Joe was in charge of collecting the money. Mikey managed circulation since he already had an afternoon paper route with the *Times*.

Like any good buck private, I had no idea I was being exploited.

During the big polio epidemic of the 1950s, everything from Double Bubble Gum to indoor theaters had been targeted as a cause of the disease. It seemed to hit especially hard in Miami, but maybe it just seemed that way because we lived near Variety Children's Hospital, where the polio victims were taken. We had seen too many of our classmates end up in iron lungs or on crutches not to take the epidemic seriously. Of course Mother, the professional worrier, had a regular health routine and set of precautions for us to ward off the disease. Even Dad agreed we had to be careful.

Knowing naps were out of the question, my parents persuaded us to stay indoors during the hottest part of the day for one entire summer. Thus, the clubhouse became the site of the longest Monopoly game ever recorded, at least in the vicinity of 58th Avenue and 38th Court. Two participants sat cross-legged at either end of Joe's bed, and one participant took a turn at kneeling on the linoleum.

At some point in the game, we decided it would be more fun to prolong it than to win it, so we created devices to keep an opponent from going bankrupt. We made loans. We negotiated elaborate land trades. We even printed stocks and bonds to make the game just a little more exciting. Shares of Amalgamated Aviation were bought and sold as easily as the deeds to Baltic Avenue or Park Place.

We managed to make the game last all summer, two or three hours a day. The board and our assets were carefully stored on the workbench each evening, and honor bound us not to tamper with each other's assets.

We were not always a completely compatible threesome. At some point during the Monopoly marathon—I think it was when I insisted on exchanging the dog token for the shoe token for good luck several times in one afternoon—my brother's patience disappeared, and I was both blasted and enchanted when he sputtered out, "Go to hell. Go directly to hell. Do not pass Go. Do not collect $200!"

My mouth dropped open in awe, and my eyes filled with tears of pride—I considered Joe the consummate linguistic genius, the master of theme swearing.

I don't know who won or lost the marathon game, or even if it really ended. None of us, however, contracted polio that summer.

Chapter 23

"Of the terrible doubt of appearances,
Of the uncertainty after all. . ."
        - Walt Whitman

Bob and Sheila Rose lived down the block a few houses, and Sheila was one of Mother's close friends. They had no children of their own, and seemed to enjoy it when any of us three children stopped at their front porch. Bob was the kind of man who kept his glasses on his head with a perpetual scowl, a grimace, and it gave him a perpetually bewildered look. The look was appropriate because his most outstanding trait was mistaking people. It didn't matter how long he'd known you—everyone was at his mercy, even me, Mercy. He was an equal opportunity mistake artist, names being as at risk as faces. When Laurie Ann moved in across the street from him, I finally had a girl in the neighborhood my own age, and he regularly mistook us for one another. Sometimes we showed up together, and he stammered until he got any two names out.

"Hey, there, Laurie. Hey there, Mercy Ann." Or Mary Ann or Laurie Ann or Anybody Ann.

When the Roses moved into the neighborhood, they introduced themselves to their next door neighbors, Andrea and Al Mendino. When he met Al Mendino, Bob thought he heard Almond Dino and referred to Al as Almond, both to others and to his face.

"Did you see the slick Pontiac Almond bought?" Bob asked my father one morning as they carpooled to work at Pan American World Airways. Dad just let it go, as did everyone else, because corrections didn't seem to take. No matter what instruction was given, Bob would soon revert back to his comfort zone.

"Ga'morning, Almond," he greeted his neighbor one day, months after he'd moved in. An exasperated Al finally told Bob to drop the Almond—his name was just Al. But, of course, it didn't take, and Al was lucky Bob didn't begin calling him Just Al.

Dad had stopped teaching and had gone into industry, as he called it, because there was more money to support a family. Bob worked in the same building as Dad, and the carpooling caused him to endure more than his share of cases of mistaken identity. One day at work, Bob made a bee line over to Dad's section to inform him that he'd just seen Juan Trippe, the founder of Pan Am, in the main cafeteria. He told Dad that, if he hurried, he, too, could see this international figure. Juan Trippe was about fifty-five then, and from what we could tell from the black and white pictures, he looked like any other prosperous businessman. He'd been in the US Navy and had graduated from Yale, and there was Hispanic blood in his background. Combine these factors with Bob Rose's ability to put two and two together and arrive at twenty-two, the cafeteria sighting should not have been taken seriously. However, it was almost lunch time, so Dad and a couple of his co-workers grabbed their black aluminum lunch boxes and headed over to try to catch a glimpse of Juan Trippe, the man who provided their jobs.

Upon entering the cafeteria, Dad and friends could tell there was some sort of commotion, but when they got up close to the area of interest, they saw a Cuban pilot, probably in his late twenties, in a sort-of Navy-ish looking uniform, holding an ice bag to his head. A rubber-gloved cafeteria worker was running around telling everyone that the poor man had stumbled over an electrical cord and had gotten that goose egg and cut on his noggin from just ONE TRIP.

"Ahh, yes," Dad commented, "One trip—Juan Trippe." Dad and friends slunk back to their section and ate their bologna sandwiches and drank their tepid coffee, shaking their heads in silent amazement.

My parents ruled out a case of early senile dementia, because the other areas of Bob's life did not seem to suffer from poor memory—he didn't find a book in his refrigerator like Miss Lily told me she once did—he just couldn't discriminate features well enough to greet people accurately, and we always had a list of situation-saving comments to smooth over his embarrassing faux pas.

"Oh, hi, Mr. Rose. It's me, Mercy."

"He really does look like Mr. Peterson, doesn't he."

"Actually, I think she's much prettier than Rita Hayworth." Not that Rita Hayworth generally hung around 58th Avenue.

Maybe it was television. There were so many new faces to digest and recall. If anyone had a distinguishing feature, say a need for orthodonture or a large nose or blue-framed glasses, the person was at special risk for being mistaken for someone else with a need for braces, rhinoplasty, or less-conspicuous optical aides.

We bumped into Bob and Sheila one evening at Rexall's when we stopped for an ice cream cone after a trip to Richard's Department Store's Friday sale. Bob motioned Mother and Dad over and mumbled that Steve Peterson must be stepping out on Sondra—he'd just seen him with that blond in the far booth. Steve was in the restroom, but was due out soon. My father wanted to leave immediately, but we children whined convincingly enough about having been promised ice cream cones that Mother and Dad finally just slipped into the booth with the Roses and positioned themselves so as not to cause recognition or embarrassment when the possibly philandering Steve reappeared. Joe and Faith and I climbed onto fountain stools and gave Lurleen our order and waited for whoever was going to exit the restroom. It was, of course, not Steve Peterson. It was some other red-haired husband.

"He really does look like Mr. Peterson," I heard Mother tell Sheila.

Lurleen Rexall rolled her eyes at me and continued scooping the chocolate into the cones.

The mistaken identity thing came to a remarkable head the night the Roses and the Malones went to the Home Show at Bay Front Park Auditorium over on Biscayne Bay. Even Bob's very tolerant wife finally declared enough was enough.

"Hi, Faith. Hi, Joe. Hi, Laurie Ann," Bob called to us children as we climbed into the back of his station wagon.

"Oh, hi, Mr. Rose. It's me, Mercy," I responded with my usual correction.

"Oh, hi, Mercy," he re-greeted me without even the slightest embarrassment visible.

We drove up Bird Road, through the Gables, and finally over the causeway to the auditorium.

"Why would Eleanor Roosevelt be at a home show?" Bob questioned no one in particular as we passed a heavy-set, curly haired, older woman in a dark lace dress in the auditorium parking lot. We had been instructed long and hard in not laughing at Bob's mistakes, but the thought of Eleanor Roosevelt's showing up to learn how to lay bathroom tile was just too rich. Luckily, the Roses and our parents couldn't hear Joe's and my smothered giggles coming from the rear of the car. Bob lacked the discernment required to rule out widows of former world leaders from Do-It-Yourself shows, but at least this time he did wonder why Mrs. Roosevelt would be present.

Inside the auditorium, we strolled up and down the long aisles of demonstration cubicles and enjoyed looking at the "Products of the Future," as they were referred to on many of the colorful banners strung across the tops of booths, but Joe, Faith, and I were really just marking time until the big talent show began at 8 p.m. We children had also been instructed to head to the stage if we got separated from the group. The master of ceremonies routinely called attention to a child on stage, announcing its name and asking for its parent to claim the usually crying youngster.

Although we thought we were all together, we looked up when the M.C. said a child named Faith was lost, and saw Bob trying to claim the little girl, who was not our Faith. She was also not blond, four years old, or of Anglo-Saxon heritage. The nearly hysterical mother ran on stage and grabbed the eight-year-old, dark-haired Cuban child from Bob and yelled something at him about kidnapping. Bob rejoined our group as if nothing happened and began examining some Formica samples.

Bob recognized and acknowledged many neighbors and Pan Am workers that night who, of course, were not neighbors or Pan Am workers. He spotted Alec Gibson, a local TV personality, who was not Alec Gibson, the local TV personality. He recognized Alec's wife Bonnie from the show, who was not Alec's wife Bonnie from the show. Some of his encounters included brief, friendly comments.

"Hey, there, Bill. Great show, huh?" Bill ignored him and moved on.

"'Evening, Mr. Simmons." Mr. Simmons ignored him and moved on.

"Well, when did you get back from Bermuda, Aunt

Mary?" Sheila, here's Aunt Mary." Aunt Mary ignored him, backed away from his attempted hug, and made a quick get away.

I expected a "Hey, there, Eleanor Roosevelt," at any moment, but it didn't happen. How hurt he must be when his friends and relatives who are not friends and relatives act like they don't know him, I thought.

Finally it was time for the talent show, and we moved forward quickly to get good seats. The first act was a three-girl singing group which called themselves "The Singing Brunettes," who Bob thought most likely were the McGuire Sisters. He kept telling us he hoped they'd sing "Sugar Time." They, of course, never did.

In all fairness, Bob did not recognize every act, but I wondered how in the world he could think the little blond tap dancing tot was Shirley Temple, who was in her mid-twenties at the time. Joe and I began naming the acts a'la Bob, and we snickered and egged each other on as we dreamed up ludicrous likenesses. The monkey riding the dog was Roy Rogers on Trigger. The tall, skinny comedian was Abraham Lincoln. The three baton twirlers with fire batons were the Three Musketeers with swords. We were too clever by half, or so we thought. Dad tapped Joe on the shoulder and told us to knock it off.

Then she appeared. Eleanor Roosevelt from the parking lot. She got up and sang "Moon Over Miami," sounding much like Kate Smith, who had made the song a national hit and a local favorite. Bob realized his mistake. She was not Eleanor Roosevelt. She was Kate Smith. He squirmed and could hardly contain himself until the song ended and he could call out, "Bravo. Encore, Kate Smith!" Eleanor-Kate smiled down at him and broke into another song. "Encore, Kate Smith!" Bob called out after the second song. He paid no attention to the master of ceremonies who thanked the singer, calling her by her stage name, Sadie from South Miami. Bob rushed over to the side of the stage to catch Eleanor-Kate and to get her autograph, which we noted as he circulated the little paper, read, Sadie from South Miami. Sheila commented about the discrepancy, and Bob snatched the autograph back and stuffed it into his shirt pocket.

During the course of the talent show, if we saw Preacher Rollo and his band, Bob saw Gene Krupa and his band. If we saw Tommy and His Trumpet Tunes, Bob saw Henry James. If we saw a local teenager dance the hula, Bob saw the lovely Hawaiian Hale Loki from *Arthur Godfrey and HIS Friends.*

Finally it was time to go home—one can handle only so many celebrities in one night—and we headed to the station wagon. Then it happened. Bob spotted two pretty little cocker spaniel pups on two leashes and informed everyone they were the Cunningham's dogs, no matter these animals were years younger than the Cunningham's nice, old cockers. Bob was already on his way to call the Cunninghams from the pay phone to tell them where their dogs were. None of us had heard that the Cunningham dogs were missing, but Bob was sure he'd stumbled on a dog-napping ring.

"That's it!" Sheila yelled as Bob headed to the phone. "STOP RIGHT NOW, BOB!" A surprised Bob stopped and turned to look at her.

Ignoring us Malones, Sheila continued, "Tonight you've seen friends who aren't friends. You've seen neighbors who aren't neighbors. You've tried to hug relatives who aren't relatives. You tried to claim that poor little Cuban girl up on stage. You spend your life seeing people you don't know, but you THINK you know. I've put up with this for ten years. I always thought you'd get it right some day. BUT I WILL NOT STAND BY AND WATCH YOU RECOGNIZE DOGS YOU DON'T KNOW!"

Bob tried to soothe Sheila, "I know I sometimes mix

people up, honey, but I don't mean to."

"You don't mean to, but you don't even TRY to get it right. Now you think you see dogs. That's it. You get it right or you get out!"

We were stunned. We were witnessing an argument in the parking lot and a threat of divorce for Bob. Dad cleared his throat and guided Mother to the far side of the car. We followed our parents and tried to hide as Sheila continued her tirade.

"Next it will be cats and rabbits and Bugs Bunny and I don't know what else," Sheila protested as she unlocked the car doors.

We all climbed in the station wagon for the silent ride home. Dad and Mother thanked Bob and Sheila for driving, and they nodded their response silently.

We worried about the Roses all day Sunday and awaited Dad's return from work on Monday so we could gain an update.

"Well, what did he say?" Mother asked. She had made a point of not calling Sheila for fear of seeming to pry.

"He didn't say anything," Dad replied. "But he didn't recognize anyone either."

"Do you think it's possible he'll stop that nonsense?

"I think it's a strong possibility," Dad told her.

Laurie Ann and I were walking back to her house one evening a week or so later. We were almost to the Rose's place, and we hoped Bob wasn't out on the porch. But luck was not with us—he sat there with Sheila in the chair next to his.

"Hey there, Laurie. Hey there, Mercy Ann. Have you checked to see if the Cunningham's dogs are in their yard?"

Sheila just shrugged her shoulders, patted Bob's arm and grinned at us.

"Oh, hey, Mr. Rose. It's me, Mercy," I called out.

Chapter 24

"They dined on mince, and slices of quince,...
and...danced by the light of the moon."
- Edward Lear

I felt good about myself when I got home from Ohio. How could a girl who'd been treated with amazing kindness and attention Up North be unimportant? I'd spent the summer swimming in our pool, reading in my room, running around the neighborhood with Joe and Mikey, and preparing for school in the fall. Actually, there wasn't much to do except check to make sure I'd grown taller and to rearrange my clothes in the dresser drawers and in the closet. There I put my second pair of penny loafers on the top shelf where a cute little toddler couldn't use her pudgy fingers to ruin my shoes again. I'd come home from Ohio with self-confidence, but like Icarus, I was flying too close to the sun.

The telephone call came on a Sunday afternoon the following spring. We'd been to church, had eaten our big dinner, and were in the living room, digesting the beef and Yorkshire pudding and every word in the Sunday *Herald* when the phone rang. Long distance calls brought the same anxious response as the frightening telegrams that arrived on light yellow paper. Mother answered, but we heard only half of what was said, and her voice was full of anxiety.

"Hello? Yes, operator, it is. Hello? Edna? What's the matter?" Then her words were strangled with sobs, and I imagined the worst—Uncle John had finally been caught by the F.B.I. and was going to hang from the neck until dead.

Mother continued, "Oh, no, what did he say exactly? Where is she now? Does she know? Should I come up?"

I realized that something must have happened to my grandmother. My father, a take-charge person who wanted the details, took the telephone away from Mother, who collapsed on her bed. Looking up and seeing me in tears, she questioned me abruptly. "What are you crying about?" We both needed comforting, and once again we turned away from each other to find it.

I went to my room, found the can of coconut I'd hidden in the back of the closet for just such occasions, and once again found tremendous solace in the crunchy sweetness. It was easier than trying to voice my feelings to my parents. Hiding in the darkness of the closet, I began telling God how sorry I was for pestering everyone about Uncle John. I felt that was probably the horrible thing I'd done to cause the crisis.

We learned that Grandmother had inoperable cancer somewhere in her stomach and would not live very long. Dad made arrangements for Mother and Faith to fly to New York on his Pan Am employee's pass, and then to take a domestic flight to Youngstown. Dad would take Joe and me up when school was out in June. I was devastated. I'd been the little princess when I was in Ohio the previous year. I'd had two women to care for me and to anticipate my needs. Now I was to stay behind and, as my parents put it, be the lady of the house. I was to quit ballet lessons and choir because there would be no transportation after school. They promised me a new school blouse if I'd stop crying, but I couldn't accommodate them.

Mother and Faith left, and we tried to go about our regular activities. Joe and I were sent to the Miller's house down the block to spend two hours after school before Dad got home from work. It was a casual household. We ate cookies out of the bag and we played Bingo and we ate potato chips out of the bag and we played Bingo. We ran in and out of the house and slammed the screen door and we drank all the Kool-Aid we wanted and we hollered indoors and we played Bingo. It was the best babysitter we ever had.

Joe and my father and I pulled together. The three of us had always joked around and liked being tougher, but this difficult time seemed to strengthen our relationship further. We developed a routine, which excluded much of the housework my mother felt so important. Only daily chores such as washing dishes were tended to. And I did know how to iron pretty well, but the bed linens were no longer changed weekly, and laundry piled up and mildewed. We had a reprieve when vacuuming was put on hold, and bathing was optional since we swam regularly.

Joe and I were told not to report this or anything else which may be upsetting to Mother, either by letter or by the very few phone calls made during the separation. Not upsetting Mother was a never-ending challenge to my father and me. Dad needn't have worried about the phone calls because I couldn't talk with my mother without choking up and becoming unable to speak. Joe did well on the phone, making it sound as if everything couldn't be better, and Dad took to quoting Shakespeare, "From you have I been absent in the spring." I thought this an appropriate choice since it seemed to combine a nice sentiment in Pennsylvania Dutch sentence structure.

Several neighbors and friends offered to come take care of the house whenever we needed it, but I don't think Dad knew what it was we needed. He'd always been happy to leave those decisions up to the women.

Cooking was something he also associated with women, and I was the only one in the house. Forget fancy Sunday dinners, we were talking survival grub only. Dad developed a menu I was to execute on a daily basis: some kind of fried meat, mashed potatoes, some kind of canned vegetable, and a dish he called grass, based on how the shredded cabbage looked in the little cellophane bags at the grocery store. I added one half cup of mayonnaise, a half cup of milk, and a tablespoon each of sugar and vinegar to the cabbage mixture to fulfill our salad requirement. It became our joke, and Joe would come in, look at the table and groan, "Oh, no. Not grass." Sometimes he'd be a wise guy, as my father called it, and he'd rub his stomach, exclaiming, "Oh, boy! Grass!" We came to expect some sort of dramatic comment from Joe, and it set a jovial tone for our meals. Fried hamburger patties, fried pork chops, fried ham steak. And then on Fridays, no-meat days, Dad picked up a pizza on his way home from work from the Italians who, it was rumored, were former mafia brothers. Dad said there were no former mafia, and the pizzeria was probably a front for more sinister dealings than pepperoni and cheese.

After several weeks, Dad decided we needed some variety in our meals and instructed me in making my first pot of spaghetti. He told me how to fry the meat and how to boil the water. We'd add the canned tomatoes later. Boiling the water sounded easy. And to save time, I added the spaghetti first while the water was still cold. In the meantime, I smooshed the ground beef into the bottom of the Revereware aluminum pan and turned the electric range to the highest setting—I was hungry and wanted to eat as quickly as possible. Soon the pan was sputtering and splattering with the juicy steam. Taking the spatula and turning over a large section of meat, I let it flop up on the side of the pan sending drops of boiling grease up into the air and onto my chest and arms.

Those were the days of little halter tops for little girls—Dad called them steering wheel covers—and there was plenty of chest and arms exposed. In my panic, I knocked the whole

144

pan onto the linoleum floor, making the grease run across the kitchen like meandering streams from a smoldering volcano. I ran outside to find Joe or Dad. Joe was impressed with the mess, including the sludge of spaghetti in the bottom of the pot, and Dad was devastated at my burned torso. He realized he'd left me with a chore beyond my capabilities. It looked so easy when Mother cooked it.

I was taken next door to Mrs. Miller's house for first aid and an inspection of my tiny chest. We had grass and peanut butter sandwiches for dinner that night, and I was spotted for a few weeks as the burns healed. Dad took over the cooking, but I was allowed to keep packing sandwiches for lunches.

———

Soon it was Easter—the weather was mild and sunny, and the church was beautiful with the strong scent of white lilies and the palm fronds and the songs. Afterward, we drove over to South Miami from Coral Gables and entered Howard Johnson's, like the Rockefellers out to the Waldorf—dressed up, full of the spirit.

The waitress saw a group of three with no woman in the party and began flirting outrageously with Dad, except I didn't know the term at the time. I just knew she was smiling too much, laughing too much, and winking too much. Not a good waitress, I judged. Not like a Rexall. Being the staunch Catholic-turned-High-Church Episcopalian, Dad felt obligated to inform the waitress as to the whereabouts of Mother, and the attention quickly subsided. We ordered Easter ham with all the trimmings, and awaited our feast.

People watching fascinated me, and I spent the time admiring the Easter outfits of the ladies around us. White hat and shoes and gloves, pink dress. Very nice. Tan suit, brown shoes, no hat. Not so nice. Straw hat with dark blue ribbons, summer print dress, sandal high heels. Very, very nice. Easter was a visually satisfying holiday.

As dinner arrived and was set before us, Joe groaned, "Grass." There it was—the tiny dish of coleslaw on each plate. We couldn't get away from it, even on Easter. Yummy ham, yummy sweet potatoes, yummy rolls, tolerable cole slaw, yucky spinach. Dad said we didn't have to eat it, which was fortunate since Joe had pointed out my spinach was beginning to dance. I gasped as the olive-colored leaf continued its gyrations, and Dad decided it was a worm. The waitress said she'd tell the cook, and asked if I'd like another bowl. Well, no, I thought, that won't be necessary.

Joe had been instructed at home on how to pay the bill—Dad felt the dinner a good opportunity for a young man to expand his social skills. Joe had practiced computing the 10% tip several times before our big dinner out, and when the check arrived, Dad gave him money, enough to more than cover the bill and the tip. Dad watched as Joe approached the waitress at the cash register, secure that his son would handle the transaction accurately. However, Joe assumed Dad was leaving the tip under the plate as he'd seen him do in the past, and put the change in his pocket.

When we stopped to see the Rexalls and to get ice cream cones, Joe and Dad realized no tip had been left for the waitress. When I suggested we drive back and hand the waitress her tip, Dad said it wouldn't look right. I had no idea why. I spent no time worrying about it—I had chocolate ice cream to devour. Murleen Rexall helped Dad reconcile his conscience, saying it was a small price for them to pay for our not making a big fuss over the spinach.

Back home, we spent the afternoon digesting our feast and wondering how Mother and Faith had celebrated Easter. They hadn't. Grandmother had dressed up, hoping to go to church one last time, but the preparations had exhausted her, and all she could do was sit in the living room, wearing the yellow rose corsage Aunt Edna had bought for the event, and look outside at the lilies of the valley blooms and the beautiful Easter Day. It was the last time she ever went downstairs or got dressed.

Chapter 25

"...Grizabella, the Glamour Cat"
- T.S. Eliot

June was getting close, the weather was getting warmer, and we needed a diversion from our Spartan, bachelor-style lives. The invitation to the beach trip was most welcome—we hadn't been to the ocean since Mother and Faith had left. My parents' friends, the Kings, were planning a Sunday car caravan over the Tamami Trail to the Gulf Coast. Destination: Naples, a tiny town in the 1950s, with the most beautiful beach and the most gentle water known, at least to us.

The Kings told Dad they were asking several other families also to join the caravan, and for us not to worry about food—they'd provide enough for both families, but Dad wanted to show his appreciation and wanted to contribute to the expense of the trip. Although the invitation had come several weeks in advance, it wouldn't have mattered if it had come only a few hours in advance. Dad, not a domestic organizer, waited until around four o'clock the day before to get us and the meal ready. Even though it was just a day trip, there were still lots of details to attend to.

"Okay, kids, let's get this show on the road," Dad commanded as he rubbed his hands together. He needed that phrase to start something as overwhelming as putting three people in bathing suits and getting in the car. Joe just sat on the sofa with his head in his latest *Superman* comic book.

"We'll put everything on the dining room table so we

don't forget anything tomorrow. Where are the beach towels?"

Beach towels? Doesn't he remember we're half Pennsylvania Dutch? Our beach towels are our oldest bath towels. The ones that had started to fray at the ends, the logic being that if you took a good bath towel or one of those large, expensive, comfortable, bona fide beach towels we didn't own to the beach, it may somehow disappear or get mustard on it or otherwise throw you into unrecoverable poverty. I rummaged around in the linen closet and found three towels bad enough for a trip to the beach. Joe continued reading.

"How 'bout bathing suits?" Dad continued.

What about bathing suits? We each had only one, and they were hanging on the little clothes line on the back porch, just like they always were. It was such a pain, just having one suit—the struggle to get into a wet bathing suit was the down side of having your own pool. I pulled our three suits off the line and slung them onto the table.

"Dad, my suit's crawling up on me again, and I HATE it," I whined.

"Well, let's take a look. I haven't noticed anything wrong with it."

I went to my bedroom and fought with the damp, uncooperative monster until I finally got into it.

"Oh, it's too short," Dad, the fashion expert, judged. "You need a new one."

"Yippee! I get a new suit. When can I get it?"

Having no concept of how much a little girl's bathing suit cost, he handed me five dollars.

"Go up to Holly's and see what they have," he generously offered.

"Come with me, Joe," I begged. "You can help me pick it out.

"I'm not going to buy a girl's bathing suit. I gotta finish *Superman*," Joe informed me, like it was for a book report or something.

I changed back into my shorts and shirt and ran as fast as I could up to Holly's Five and Dime to begin the search for my dream suit.

"Hey, there, little girl," the old lady behind the counter said, "Whatcha need today?"

"I need a bathing suit," I proudly explained, waving the five dollar bill in the air." Gloria Swanson could not have emoted more dramatically.

What size do I wear? Hmm. That's a good question. I wasn't aware of sizes, only if things fit or didn't.

"I'm nine, so I guess I wear a nine."

"They don't make nines. Do you wear an eight or a ten?"

This was beginning to get hard. What would Gloria Swanson say?

"I'm nine, but I'm short. Maybe an eight?" I suggested.

"Well here's this little blue one with a fish on the front. Isn't this cute?" she wondered.

Well, ya, if you're a baby, I thought.

I began digging through the suits myself, but could find nothing appropriate for a girl of nine who wanted to look older. Then I saw it—a tiny neon pink two-piece with black designs on the top. It was nothing more than some patches of fabric and lots of strings for ties, top and bottom. I'd seen pictures of the new little bathing suits, but had never seen one up close.

"I like this one," I announced to the saleslady.

"Oh, hon, that's a lady's bikini. It's on sale, but you can't wear it."

"Well, since I'm little, it won't look so small on me," I insisted as I gave her my five dollars and waited for the change.

A bathing suit on sale—Mother will be so proud of me, and it's hard to outgrow a two piece with strings. A very wise investment. Yes.

When I got home, Joe was still sitting on the sofa with Superman, and Dad was trying to figure out how to make a meat loaf, Mother's standard sandwich meat for beach picnics.

"Wait 'till ya see what I got," I gushed as I ran to my room to change. The top of the suit tied at my neck and midriff, and the bottom had lace up ties at each side, which I pulled as tightly as I could to keep it up.

Slinking back down the hallways like the girls in the Miss Florida contest on TV, I asked, "Well, how do you like it?"

Dad and Joe looked up, and I guess it was Dad that gasped first. Joe gave his I've-been-whiplashed jerk of the head and focused on the top of the suit.

"What are those things on the top?" he asked, referring to the beautiful decorations.

"They're seahorses—see how their stomachs stick out?"

"Probably male seahorses," Dad mumbled.

"They're not seahorses," Joe exclaimed in glee, "they're bathing beauties leaning back!" Finally something more interesting than Superman.

"They're just designs, just decorations," I countered.

"Well, why does the suit stick out?" he snickered.

"It's a lady's suit. I got it on sale," I bragged, swelling my chest and trying to fill the gaping cups.

"Whoa, there, Mercy. You can't wear that," Dad finally sputtered as he focused in on the details of the suit. "It's not decent."

"It covers me up, and it doesn't crawl up and hurt like my old one," I protested like a desperate lawyer.

"No, take it back to Holly's and get another one. A decent one," he commanded.

This time Joe didn't mind going to the store with me. He held the suit in his hands an inappropriately long time before telling the saleslady, "She can't keep this."

"Well, I'm sorry, hon," the saleslady began, "we can't take bathing suits back. It's against the law."

"She only had it on for about ten minutes," Joe countered. No chance now to pretend I hadn't worn it. Or was that his plan?

"I'm sorry, I tried to warn her," the saleslady informed Joe in an attempt to prevent a contributing-to-the-delinquency-of-a-minor violation on her conscience. "If I take it back, I get in trouble with the owner, and the store gets in trouble. We just can't take it back."

Joe shrugged, and we left. I was jubilant. No dumb fish on a baby suit—a real bathing suit, and I got it on sale.

Dad phoned the lady at Holly's, and she re-explained the law. She also told him she assumed I was buying it for a present for my mother. Nice cover, I thought, and grinned, knowing the suit was legally mine now. I laid it on the table and wisely turned Dad's attention to the pressing matter of meatloaf, and Joe went back to Superman—he was now on his third reading.

"We'll eat a big breakfast before we leave in the morning and stretch the meatloaf into two meals of sandwiches. What else? Mother always made a casserole of baked beans and packed jars of water and lemonade and a thermos of coffee for you. Just add some oranges, and we'll have our picnic," I assured Dad.

It was getting late, and I was sent to B-Thrifty's for two pounds of hamburger, a big can of beans, and oranges. We already had lots of bread and plenty of lemons. Joe couldn't go to the store with me—he was on his fourth reading.

While I was shopping, Dad began formulating the meatloaf recipe, which he imagined was like making meatballs, only bigger. Joe remembered Mother put corn flakes in the meat mix, and onions and eggs and milk and something else. When I got back from the store, I couldn't remember what the other ingredient was. I just knew I liked it. Oh, yes, it was catsup. We'll use lots of catsup.

Dad cut up three onions into huge wedges. I looked for the corn flakes, but we were out. B-Thrifty's was now closed, but we did have raisin bran. We all liked raisin bran. We needed four eggs for breakfast, so there was only one left for the meatloaf, but we did have lots of milk. Dad thought himself a natural chef, although he had very little experience cooking. Who needs to measure? Who needs a recipe? We began assembling:

Two pounds of hamburger
Three onions
Half a box of raisin bran
One egg
Two cups of milk
A cup of catsup.

Now mix it all up and bake it in the glass loaf pan. There was too much meat mix for one loaf pan, so Dad brought out another. With all the catsup and milk and raisins and onion wedges, the whole mess looked like an autopsy gone bad.

"Okay," Dad calculated, "this should cook for an hour. I think."

It was 6:30, and we hadn't had dinner, what with being so busy assembling tomorrow's feast. Dad had exhausted his culinary repertoire for the evening, so we agreed on peanut butter sandwiches and grass for a quick meal. We made jars of lemonade, and waited for the oven timer to go off. . .DING!

First check, 7:30 p.m. Both pans were still soggy. Reset the temperature to broil and watch the *Jackie Gleason Show* on TV. I danced around the living room in my ballet slippers as if I were a member of the June Taylor Dancers, and we laughed big belly laughs at the clever antics of Ralph and Alice and Ed Norton—Trixie wasn't in the skit that night...DING!

Second check, 8:30 p.m. Both pans were black on top, but red at the bottom. Turn the temperature down to 200 degrees. Back to the TV. *Your Hit Parade* came on, and I sang along with Snooky Lansen and Dorothy Collins, whose mouth Dad said looked like a bird's. I knew most of the words to the musical hits, so Joe's suggestion of my pantomiming the songs seemed reasonable to me—I was disturbing his sixth reading of the *Superman* comic. Dad was relaxing in his chaise lounge in the Florida room, and in an instant, like Faith's Jack-in-the-box, he bolted out of his chair and yelled to no one in particular, "I didn't bake the beans."

"We don't have to bake them," Joe suggested, not wanting to interfere with his own leisure time. "We'll just eat them out of the can, like cowboys do." Dad was proud of his ingenious son, and collapsed once again on the green chaise.

Joe and I were sent to bed at 9:30, after the third oven check, but wrangled it up to 10:00 to finish watching *Gunsmoke*, and Dad continued waiting for the meatloaf to cook all the way through.

I got up around midnight to get a drink of water and found Dad asleep in the lounge chair. I told him it was time for him to go to bed, and once again, Jack sprung up out of the box.

"Where's the meatloaf?" he demanded.

"I don't know," I answered honestly.

The meatloaf pans were in the oven, totally black on top, and a nice shade of blush-tan on the bottom. They'd finally cooked through and through. It was then we remembered the catsup was supposed to go on top of the dish, not in it. Dad reset the alarm clock—he knew we wouldn't make it to church after our long, hard night.

The next morning, we put shorts and shirts on over

our bathing suits, and I left my blouse hanging open, just in case someone wanted to look at my bikini. We packed everything into paper bags and drove out to the King's house to join the caravan.

The Kings had invited two other families, and the four cars proceeded west on the Tamiami Trail, the only road to Naples in those days. The drive paralleled the canal, which also ran from Miami to Naples, and we watched carefully for alligators on the roadside or on the bank. That morning's tally was three, long, checkerboard-skinned reptiles. No fair counting the huge pieces of truck tires, which the guys called road gators.

As we continued through the Everglades, we were able to see the Seminole Indians sitting in their chickees. The houses were four poles with an elevated platform floor and a palmetto frond thatched roof. The Seminoles were in the traditional costume—brightly colored long skirts and long-sleeved blouses, and long-sleeved shirts for men. Summer or winter, long sleeves were necessary to keep the mosquitoes at bay. I admired the women's hair, which was glossy black and brushed up into a large, smooth roll at the top of the head. On a lesser cultural level, we could also watch the road speed by under our car, through the rusted-out holes in the floor of The Old Chevy. Ahh, the salt air.

After two hours on the road we arrived in Naples, and the four families got out of the cars and assembled for introductions and play. All-in-all, there were seven adults, Dad being the only single, and six children. Taking off my shirt and shorts and sandals, I ran to the shore. I could hear Dad telling the grown-ups about my bathing suit, but I was too beautiful and grown up and ready to swim to lag behind to listen.

The water in Naples was warm and gentle—you could stand with the surf up to your chest and jump the rolling waves for hours. You could sit at the shoreline and let the waves nudge you back and forth, to and fro. You could walk out on the pier to monitor the day's catch, and you could work up an appetite.

Billy, one of the King boys, was on the large side. He had brought a small beach chair and preferred sitting in it, rather than swimming. When he'd get up, the chair would stick to his hips, and he'd wander around with it attached like a Victorian lady's bustle. Watching his impressive performance, I wondered how one person could be so efficient.

"Come on in, kids," Dad eventually called from the blanket. "Let's eat."

With pride, he pulled out a meatloaf pan, the bread, the can of beans, and everything else. He sawed away at the brick of sandwich meat until he had some moderately edible pieces. While I shook catsup on my bread, Joe began the traditional catsup-shaking poem, projecting in a stilted, classical actor's way, "Shake, shake the catsup bottle. None will come, and then a lot'll." That Joe, so handsome and smart, and so clever. He'll really go far in life, I mused.

Dad poked the huge can of beans with the little can opener and cranked it around until he could pull the jagged top back. With one of Mother's sterling silver tablespoons, he dipped huge scoops onto our paper plates, cowboy style. He circulated the can among the other guests. Oddly, all declined. He passed the loaf pan of meat around, too. Oddly, all declined. But they did like the lemonade, and Billy, who with wagging rear chair appendage had come to sit next to us, took two oranges.

"I like your bathing suit, Mercy," he began.

"Yeah, the seahorses are cute," I replied.

"Those aren't seahorses," Joe informed him like a big brother would, "Look closer."

"That's enough for lunch now, kids," Dad interjected before Billy could focus on the well-endowed bathing beauties. Let's swim."

That's funny, I thought. He usually makes us wait a half hour before going back in the water. Billy wagged over to someone else's blanket and accepted more lunch handouts.

We swam too much that day, jumped too many waves, ate too much, played in the sun too long, left for home too late, and generally had a fabulous time. We hadn't had such a good outing since Mother had gone north, and we understood when Dad said that sometimes a change of scenery does one good.

The next morning I awoke with a sunburn that outlined my bikini, and when Mother saw me in Ohio later that summer, she asked how I got such a funny tan line.

I wore the bikini at home for a few more weeks, and I have no idea where or when it was removed from the house, although Dad said something about a laundry accident. Before we headed north, he presented me with a new one-piece suit, size ten to allow for growth, with pink and white checks and lace around the top. It was no where near so glamorous as the one with the bathing beauties.

Chapter 27

"You don't love someone for their looks, or their clothes...
But because they sing a song only you can hear."
- Anonymous

Dear Advice to the Lovelorn Editor,

What with Valentine day comin up, I thought some a yer gal readers mite be likin some advice on how to catch a man. Romanse is in the air.

I done told you me and sis grew up on the farm up north so I was just lucky that Mr. Roy DeWitte James showed up at our door one day and told Mama he'd jus like to marry one of us gals. He done seen us at the livestock auction when we took our Lulubelle to be sold to slaughter. He said he just leaned back on the bleachers at the auction and watched us cane the hogs around the ring and knew he wanted a gal with grace. Looks was not enough. Well Mama said it better be Bertha because sis done alreddy told Mr. Leonard "Lucky" Crabtree that she'd marry him when he got rid of his still cause she wouldn't marry no potential convict. Well Mr. Roy DeWitte James said I was jus fine and when could we get married? Mama done said we had to finish up school and 8 grade would be up in June. So I was a June bride. Romanse was in the air then too. Well when me and the Mr. had our little Bobbie Suette we didn't have a lot of money like we do now but I always got Aunt Theola Thurlows old magazines and I done learnt a lot about etiquette by a readin them. I knew if we wanted Bobbie Suette to marry well she'd have to have grace like I done with them hogs but we didn't raise no hogs, me and the Mr. So we'd just have to work on her in other ways. In one issue of "Betsy's Book for the Ladies" was an article about finishing schools and how they done worked on them gals there with the graces of playin a instrument and speakin a different language like Frenchy or Italy or Latin or something. A gal also needed to be a knowin about getting an education. Well when Bobbie Suette was a growin up we done start makin our own finishing school for her. We decided she would graduate high school and everything. We then started her on learnin an instrument but we didn't have no money for none. Well Mr. Roy DeWitte James has a good brian in his head and he done brought in a bicycle innertube from the shed and showed Bobbie Suette how to let the air out a the valve a little at a time and play tunes. Playin tunes out of a innertube is a good skill that can be kept all yer life not like a twirlin a baton or something. Bobbie Suette done got real good at a playin "Always" on the innertube without havin to pump air back in with her foot pump before the song was over. "I'll be lovin you ALWAYS with a love that's true ALWAYS." It was so beautiful that it done brought tears to our eye. We talked to the principal at the school but they didn't offer no language except English so we just had to do what we could. Aunt Theola Thurlow's big boy Darrell DeWayne Thurlow has a boy hisself named

Mervyn what done speak Pig Latin. Well it wouldn't be no real fancy Latin but we done thought it wood be close enough and isn't it funny that my grace was hogs and one a Bobbie Suettes graces would be PIG Latin. I guess it's in the jeans. Ha. Ha. Ha. She done learned "Always" in Pig Latin real good and at high school graduation talent night she got up on stage and played her innertube which the Mr. had shined up real good special for the night with a little Oleo. I also tied some ribbons onto the pump. She sang her little heart out. "I-way ill-way e-bay oving-lay oo-yay ALWAYS. " Well she done brought down the house and Bubba L. Bigelow and Bubba G. Bigelow caught me and the Mr. out in the parkin lot and said they wanted to marry Bobbie Suette. Well we know all our hard work with languages and instruments had paid off because the Bubba Boys father was the owner of the Five Teat Milking Farm down to Sarasota way which was named after a cow they once had with five teats not four. We knew Bobbie Suette would be well cared for all her life what with all that money

from the teat place. The Mr. told the Bubba
Boys that they'd better choose which one got
Bobbie Suette because we didn't go in for
any of that funny business with 2 husbands
in OUR family! Bubba L. pinned Bubba G.
2 times outa 3 right there in the parkin lot
and took Bobbie Suette home in his car that
night while poor ole bloody nose Bubba G.
had to thumb a ride back to the teat place. So
if you want to catch a good man get yerself
some hogs and a cane or a innertube or some
other way to prove you have the graces so
important in a good match. Good luck to all
you valentines. Romanse is in the air.

Bertha James

Chapter 28

"This is the way the world ends,
Not with a bang but a whimper."
- T.S. Eliot

Some psychologists feel what occurs when children are ten years old is pivotal the rest of their lives. I spent the summer between fourth and fifth grades in Ohio, watching my grandmother die.

We stayed in Grandmother's home, and we children were encouraged to spend as much time as possible out of doors or in the cellar so that my mother and a nurse could minister to Grandmother by day, and my mother and young aunt could minister to her by night. I didn't bother Grandmother about any more Grace stories—she knew I could recite the catechism and that I would pass it down to my own daughter some day. The closeness we'd developed the year before would be with us forever, and she would never have to talk about Uncle John again. I did wonder how he would fit into the household crisis. Joe said not to worry, he wouldn't be coming home.

But I knew more about family dynamics than Joe did, or so I thought. I imagined Uncle John would come out of hiding, would don a disguise, and would knock on the door soon to see his mother before she left her earthly world. I imagined the disguise would be the total opposite of how he normally looked, so any taller man with light hair who came to the door was suspect, especially the mailman. What a perfect cover, I thought, delivering mail and being able to check up on things at the same time. I made myself available during the daily delivery, and even followed "Mr. Brown" occasionally to see if he passed the heavy letter bag off to the real mailman when he rounded the corner.

Grandmother was a popular teacher, if not with all of the students, with all of their parents. She was a respected Presbyterian, a member of a large extended family, and a good neighbor. When she became ill, armloads of gladiolas, roses, and snapdragons arrived, and as they began to wilt, my mother would take the tall vases down to the back porch. There I would sit in the early morning sun, sorting and salvaging the still-living blossoms from the dead and dying. It was a sanctuary. On the back porch, the sickness and needles and moaning and ice chips were another world away, and they could not touch me. But it was on the back porch that the horrible reality of Grandmother's illness finally sunk in. The decayed flower stems had the same funny smell as her bedroom. Like the beautiful blooms, she was fading away.

It was also my job to take the get well cards upstairs after the morning delivery and read them to Grandmother. These were brief, but nice, moments between us. Grandmother had been bathed and brushed and helped into a clean nightie and bed jacket. The linens had been changed and the bedroom redded up. The temperature upstairs was still somewhat cool, and that early summer morning feeling made everyone feel fresh and hopeful.

My mail visits often brought smiles to Grandmother's drawn face. I wasn't very good at deciphering some cursive writing, so I told her one card was sent from Jazabel. I was familiar with that name because my father often used it to describe my sister or myself when we behaved in a less-than-puritanical manner. Grandmother laughed out loud, her last long laugh, and told me, "That's Isabel, Snickle Fritz. That's the lady your mother is named after." I was delighted with her laughter and with the term of endearment, which I liked to think she reserved just for me.

Joe and I had been told our grandmother did not know she was dying. In those days, the terminally ill often were not told the truth. True lies of mercy. Graceful offers of hope. But when a well-meaning friend wrote on a card that Grandmother was not going to get well and that it was terrible that no one was telling her, I quickly changed the message to words of rapid recovery and ran down stairs to show my mother the awful card. It was then the family decided the time had come for reality.

Befitting the occasion, my mother and young aunt dressed up early one evening and sent us out to play in the back yard. Joe and I sat in the long shadows of the vegetable garden, keeping Faith out of trouble. When we saw the minister's car drive up, we moved to the side of the house under our grandmother's open window, sitting on the cool slate side steps and mindlessly toying with the remains of the lilies of the valley blooms. We knew it was a family crisis and wished our father were with us instead of, as he put it, holding down the fort in Miami. We heard the awful sobbing upstairs, and it broke our hearts.

After a respectable length of time, the minister left and Mother appeared, her face red and her eyes swollen. She clutched a twisted, wet hankie and told us Grandmother had been the brave one. She said that, if Jesus thought it the right time to die, then she was fine with his decision. Grandmother had only been concerned about her children and felt glad they were settled into their lives. Mother was married. Aunt Edna was working at a good job. Nothing more could be done for Uncle John. Nothing more could be done for Uncle John? Did Grandmother have a hand in his dodging the F.B.I.? Does she know that he shows up every morning around 9 to hand me the mail? Does she know that his disguise makes him look more like a German, with that light brown hair? I felt it soon would be time to take a stand and confront "Mr. Brown," the mailman. If he wanted to see his mother before she died, he'd better act quickly.

That evening, Joe stayed outdoors looking for the kids next door, and Faith and I bathed and went to bed in the room next to Grandmother, who made no sound to upset us.

There was a feeling of belonging in her neighborhood. With no air conditioning, and with the cool air only creeping in before dawn, windows were left open and the sounds crept up and down the street, night and day.

Ours was not the only house monitoring Grandmother's decline. Support was coming from folks who had also grown up in the neighborhood--folks who knew she was dying in that upstairs bedroom that faced the street, and there was a respectful quiet on the block befitting the process.

The rest of the summer passed in a blur of childhood activity mixed with grown up grief. We played quietly during the increasing bad times, and Grandmother got down to the practicality of planning her funeral during the decreasing good times.

"The neighbors will bring side dishes," she whispered, dictating notes as my mother wrote on the back of a used envelope. "But we'll need the main dish. A ham or turkey. Ham will be better, easier to cook. See if Mrs. Thompson next door will come over and stay at the house that morning. She can put the ham on and make sure everything is arranged, and watch Faith, too. She can watch her house and our house at the same time." Grandmother lay back, exhausted but pleased with the progress. Then another day she continued, "Make sure the buffet is set with the Haviland china. Maybe Mercy and Joe will polish the silver for you. Put the leaves in the table. The long tablecloth is in the bottom drawer of the buffet. Better check it for yellow spots—we haven't used it since Christmas. Just soak it in lots of water and a little Clorox if you find any spots. On other days, Grandmother chose which dress to be buried in and told Mother which flowers would be in bloom and used on the table.

The whole subject frightened me, and I finally asked Mother, "Why would Grandmother want to talk about dying?"

Mother replied, "She's not talking about dying. She's talking about her funeral. She's been to so many in her life that she knows just what she wants hers to be like. It will be her last party, and she's not leaving the details to amateurs." Note to myself: Plan my funeral and make sure my blue dress is ironed.

As the days shortened and the nights became cooler, my father paid a housekeeper to do a complete overhaul on our house in Miami, and he flew to Ohio to help ease the end. He struggled to inject needles through Grandmother's thickened, dehydrated skin into a body that had no muscle left to accept the painkilling drugs. He argued with the doctor about the dose and eventually begged him to provide heroin to lessen her misery, but it was not to be. Law required she suffer.

Realizing I had not much time to reunite Uncle John, who was posing as the mailman, with Grandmother, I approached "Mr. Brown" when I saw him coming up the steps to the front door one morning.

"Hello, Uncle John," I blurted out. Probably best to catch him off guard. "You can fool everyone else, but you can't fool me."

"Hello, Mercy," Mr. Brown responded. "Why did you call me Uncle John?"

"I think you know why," I retorted with a smug look on my face.

"No, I don't. Tell me."

"You think you can fool everyone, but I know who you really are.

"And who may that be?"

"My Uncle John. The Nazi spy. If you want to see Grandmother before she dies, just tell me."

With that, Mr. Brown asked to speak with Mother. "Mrs. Malone," he began as he tipped his hat to her," I think Mercy has something to tell you. Good-bye, ladies."

"What's going on, Mercy?" Mother asked.

"I think Mr. Brown is Uncle John in disguise," I responded, realizing how silly my answer sounded. "I think Uncle John wants to find out about Grandmother and how she's feeling and when she's dying," I added weakly.

"Mercy, I've told you time and again not to bother people about Uncle John. It is not your business what he is doing with his life. Just wait until I tell your father," she warned.

"But if he wants to see Grandmother, why can't he?" I demanded. Knowing my father was now involved, I needed to up my stakes.

Mother then told me the story of Uncle John. The whole story.

Mrs. Martinelli, a neighbor, had predicted that, in accordance with nature, Grace Caroline Kaufmann, our grandmother, would wither and die when the leaves began to turn in the fall, and just as the nights started to become chilly, Grandmother Grace joined the ages.

When we went home to Miami, I found myself daydreaming on my bed, remembering my grandmother and the other Graces. I could hear her say, "I was born in 1893. Born in the house behind ours, in your great-grandmother's house. I went to the school here in Niles where your mother and Aunt

Edna went. We always came home for lunch every day, and my mother would have a full dinner set for us. My father had the grocery store over on Maple Avenue, and he came home for dinner at noon, too. My father's people were farmers, and we still ate in the old way with the big meal at noon. We always had pie—apple, cherry, peach, or pumpkin—whatever was growing at the time or what we'd put up in jars in the basement. Sometimes if there was no fruit, we'd have shoo-fly pie. We made it with molasses, and it was so sweet the flies swarmed over, and we'd have to shoo them away. Why, we had pie so much, we even ate it for breakfast sometimes. Or strudel or mush or ekk bread.

"I wore dark dresses to school and sometimes an apron, just like my mother and grandmother. Sometimes the aprons were fancy, and sometimes we wore little white caps. I had the high button shoes, too, and so did your mother. I liked to watch the boys shoot steelies at school. They were like marbles, but I never got a chance to shoot them. Girls weren't allowed. When I got older, my mother said a baby was on the way, and when my sister was born, we knew we had something special. She laughed and cried and jabbered all the time. Oh, what fun we had with her. She was only seven when World War I was over, and she made herself a little paper hat and decorated her red wagon with crepe paper, and walked in the Armistice Day parade downtown with the band and open cars and wagon floats. We never knew what she'd be up to next. She was such a live wire.

"When I met your grandfather and got married, my parents gave us this house. The next year your mother was born and seven years later, Aunt Edna. She was a live wire, too."

Note to myself: Be a live wire. People seem to like it. Second note: No mention of Uncle John, now or forever.

Chapter 29

*He did not soon forget the reproachful glance
Amy gave him, as she went, without word to anyone,
straight into the ante-room, snatched her things,
and left the place forever."*
- Louisa May Alcott

Dear Helen,

How are you? I am fine. Remember last year when we started reading Little Women when I was staying next door in Ohio and Grandmother was dying? Well, I got in trouble because of it. Remember when Amy leaves school in the middle of the day because the teacher was mean to her? Well my teacher is always making fun of us and yesterday morning he said I was an odd ball because I got up out of my desk on the left side and he told us to do that and everyone else in my row got up on the right side but it is the wrong side. He hurt my feelings again so I went to the girls bathroom and went in one door and out the other and got on my bike and came home. Mother was cleaning the cupboard under the sink and had on a halter top and shorts and hadn't had her bath yet and had a roach dead on a newspaper and told me to go to bed until I stopped crying. I took an orange with me and peeled it so fast because I was so mad and crying so hard. Later about at least an hour Mr. Timothy drove up to our house and told Mother I was too sensitive and Mother said she knew that and why did it take so long for someone to call her that I was missing?

My first grade teacher Mrs. King called and told Mother that Mr. Timothy was in a lot of trouble at school. My friend Karen told me today that Mr. Timothy went back to school yesterday and told all the kids that I was too sensitive. He said nobody tell anyone what he said but Karen told me and I told Mother and Daddy and they are going to have a talk with him. He also said some of the girls in the class have been talking with lisps on purpose and that I started it which is a lie because I don't lisp and the other girls have braces and do lisp and my teeth are straight. I hate him but everybody says I am his pet but how can I be his pet when he laughed at me when I by mistake said bottom instead of body when I had to read the paragraph on digestion but all the kids were nice because they knew how embarrassed I was for making that terrible mistake. Mother was so embarrassed that he saw her in her shorts and halter top because she thought he would just call and she was mad at me. My eyes are red from crying so much. Mother says that I can have a new dress for school because this happened to me and we are going shopping on Friday at Richard's where they have a sale. I liked living next door to you in Ohio and having you in my neighborhood.

Love,

M e r c y

Carol Jo Pettit

Chapter 30

"The Awful shadow of some unseen Power
Floats . . . amongst us."
- Percy Shelly

"Choose a partner," the reporter demanded, and Joe, who was 13 at the time, automatically turned to me. As the flashbulbs cracked blue and blinded us, we posed for a photo story about our Friday night cotillion. When published, the photo caption read, "A Gentleman Also Dances with His Sister."

Serious cotillion seems to be a Southern institution, and ours was designed to prepare South Miami junior high school students for a smooth transition into the social scene. Joe, Mikey, and I attended cotillion together. There were no crushes between Mikey and me, and he and Joe maintained that friendly rivalry, so at cotillion we went our individual ways, often returning to our comfortable threesome between dances.

The evenings in Miami seemed warmer in those days, even in the winter. Our cotillion met at an outdoor pavilion every week to dance to the heavy beat of early rock and roll songs like "Rock Around the Clock", "In the Chapel in the Moonlight", and "Dance with Me, Henry." In addition to the patio, which seemed festive adorned with red and blue and yellow Japanese lanterns and the heady fragrance of flowering tropical foliage, we also had access to a lounge for rest and a snack bar for refreshment. Those were the days of energetic bopping, so lounging and refreshing sounded good several times a night.

Naturally we dressed up for the dance—it was the 50s. Allowing for growth spurts, the boys wore too-large or too-small sports coats and ties, and the girls wore too-long or too-short church and party dresses. We were transported by our parents, and on the way to cotillion, our threesome felt grown up, dignified, and sometimes confident in our best clothes. Since I was a year younger than Mikey and two years younger than Joe, we were well matched in social skills—not too good at them—just well matched.

We were changing from children to adults, and some evenings when I'd been playing endless tetherball, I'd feel the tug from both directions. My mother would give me a countdown.

"If you want to go to cotillion, Mercy," she'd warn me, "you have to come in and take a bath in fifteen...ten...five minutes...NOW!" I had to decide between whopping my way to tetherball victory and donning my pink nylon dress with three stiff crinoline petticoats and dancing the night away until 9 p.m. I always ended up choosing cotillion.

Once there, our evenings were divided into formal dance lessons, several snowball dances so that we all would meet and mingle, and free dancing. Our dance instructors were an older man of about twenty-five and a beautiful young Cuban woman who wore burgundy nail polish, gardenias in her jet black hair, and smelled of sweet jasmine. I delighted in her exotic appearance, which was such a contrast from our Midwestern conservatism.

The chaperones saw that everyone danced, and none too closely. We stumbled our way through the intricacies of the box step and the bop, the two remedial requisites for junior high social success. Later we were introduced to the mambo, the cha-cha, and the calypso. Between cotillion evenings, we three dancers would practice in Joe's room. Because of economy, he still had the cowboy and Indian linoleum, and it made for easy movement. Dance practice was a sad affair to witness. I'd had ballet lessons and was a majorette, so I'd been moving to music for years, but those two boys agonized over each step. Mikey's main problem was adolescence—he was large and clumsy. Joe's main problem was spontaneity when he tried to do the bop. With the box step, he could just count and push his partner around, like moving a chest of drawers, and at the end, if the mood struck, add the flourish of a modest dip. But the bop meant letting go, thinking on your feet, anticipating step changes, and giving your partner subtle signals when you were going to execute a twirl.

At home, I'd generally be the boys' dance partner/ victim, but sometimes they'd be desperate enough to have me observe where the problem lay. Practice would then become a series of oaths of secrecy, clomps, shoves, accusations, apologies, and very little progress.

"You have to be the girl this time...Na-uh, I had to be the girl last time...Don't kick me...Don't you kick ME...Go under my arm...No YOU go under MY arm...Don't push me... Don't push ME...Sorry...Sorry. How was that, Mercy?"

Ye, gads, I thought how much worse can this get?

I realized how urgent their need was when they eventually presented me with their new scheme: write down, memorize, and execute a planned pattern, repeating it over and over and over until the music mercifully stopped, or their partner left the floor. It went something like this: Grasp girl's right hand with my left hand. Lean toward girl. Push away with my left hand against her right hand. Do ten slide-toe moves while rocking backward. Twirl girl under my left arm. Repeat. Repeat. Repeat.

Joe and Mikey were proud that our practice sessions were much more civilized until I pointed out they would have to educate every girl they intended to dance with so that she didn't take off and do something wild or spontaneous. Oh, God, the S word.

The plan did at least give the boys the courage to do the bop, and to their credit, most girls were good enough dancers to follow the rudimentary steps.

As the months passed, we eventually knew everyone at cotillion, and with adolescent hormones raging, a few romances developed. Mine was with a klutzy-but-nice boy named Doug who asked me to dance every dance. The boys called us Grace and Graceless.

One Saturday, after an enjoyable Friday evening of dancing, Doug bicycled several miles to my house to deliver a little fifteen-cent bottle of dime store Orange Blossom cologne as a token of his love. When Doug arrived at my house, hot, sweaty, and dirty, my Friday-Night gentleman seemed less glamorous and more like the hot, sweaty, dirty boys in Phys Ed class at school. I invited Doug to sit down wind by the pool, offered him some cool lemonade, accepted the little bottle, sniffed the overpowering cologne, sneezed several times, remembered my names were mercy and grace, and voiced my appreciation.

Mikey had been in love with a classmate for years, so he made no serious alliances at cotillion—he concentrated mainly on taming his huge feet. And Joe continued to dance with this girl and that girl, usually sticking with a sympathetic partner as long as she tolerated his monotonous dance plan.

However, when fame presented itself, and Joe was chosen to be photographed for the newspaper, he automatically turned to me because, at cotillion, a gentleman also dances with his sister.

Chapter 31

"Sweet springtime is my time is your time is our time...
And viva sweet love."
- e.e. cummings

"Oh, no, Mercy," Susan whispered, "the boys know we're having a movie." Susan had left class to use the restroom and had come back with the horrifying news. What embarrassment we'd feel when we rejoined the boys next period. They had their movies and we had ours—*Your Changing Body, Becoming a Woman,* and worst of all, today's movie, *How Families are Started.*

The movies were important since most of our parents felt uncomfortable dealing with the issues of sex. Being junior high students, we reacted in a most atrocious manner—squirming, giggling, side comments the Phys Ed coach couldn't hear—anything to de-escalate the intensity of the moment.

The girls in our class brought varying degrees of information into the sessions—information gained from a sister or from an older girl in the neighborhood, and even occasionally from a responsible adult. I brought up the low end of the knowledge continuum, still thinking babies were started when the couple wished very hard for a precious bundle. So it was with great shock that, in the darkened classroom, we saw images of cows grazing in a pasture...a bull being introduced into the herd...and amazing contortion on the part of the bovine couple who were obviously going steady. Then the picture flashed to a woman in a bridal dress, a groom approaching her, a brief made-for-the-movies wedding, and finally the couple walking down the aisle. Next scene: calendar pages flying off and a new year beginning. Next scene: couple happily gazing at an infant in a bassinet. Could it be that humans started babies the way the cows did? Is this what the movie was trying to get at?

At the end of the movie, Betsy, and equally uninformed girl, shyly asked the rough and ready Phys Ed coach if humans had to go through the contortions the cows did, which brought howls of laughter from all of the girls in the room except Susan and me. The poor coach quickly yanked on the window shades, allowing streams of sunlight into the classroom, dismissed us and told us to stand out on the field until the bell rang. We poured outside with red faces and diverted eyes.

But we continued the session. There was one topic I still didn't understand—this thing about taking nine months for a baby to develop unless the pregnancy was interrupted. We weren't allowed to use the word pregnancy—it was much too clinical. Even on *I Love Lucy* they had to say *expecting*. Okay, what would interrupt an expectancy? My parents always told me not to interrupt, but this was usually when I'd butt in when Faith was trying to explain something in six-year-old words. It had to be something different. I couldn't ask Joe later—he was a boy, and we didn't talk about such things together.

I turned to Susan, "What do you think they mean about interrupting an expectancy?" She understood my terminology, coming from a family almost as conservative as mine.

"It means," she explained, "that sometimes the baby doesn't make it all the way to nine months and sometimes dies." This sounded so sad to me. Imagine thinking you were having a baby and then having it die.

Ellie, one of the more sophisticated seventh graders, added in raspy whispers, "Or you go to Cuba and a doctor stops the baby. Leslie's sister went to Cuba. She was seventeen and at

Gables High last year and got pregnant and her mother took her to Cuba, and when she came back, she wasn't pregnant. Leslie found out from her sister and wasn't supposed to tell anyone, but she told me. They weren't supposed to tell anyone in case her sister might get in trouble with the police."

We'd heard talk of girls who got married at Gables High and had babies only a few months later, but we'd never heard of going to Cuba. Very interested, Susan and I asked for further explanation, but Ellie said she shouldn't have told us, and admonished, "DON'T TELL ANYONE!" and made a quick exit.

Susan and I signaled Doris over. She seemed to know a lot about these things. She'd laughed loudest during the movie.

"It's against the law, Mercy," Doris explained. "You can't stop a baby on purpose."

"How would the doctor stop it anyway?" Susan asked.

"They give her an operation. You know, like getting your appendix taken out."

Since my parents hadn't broached even the most basic sex education with me, abortion and church doctrine and choice were way down the road. So I decided that, if a high school girl goes through the motions like the cow and ends up with a baby before she's married and can't get married, and people talk about you if a baby comes too early, then Cuba sounded like a good idea. Mother had her appendix out after Faith was born and didn't seem worse for the wear.

Note to myself: Don't go around with boys who want you to do the cow thing.

The bell rang and we went into the building where the boys were filtering into English class. A few of them had smirks on their faces. They knew we'd had the movie.

Chapter 32

"...believe me, it's the fellow with four to ten thousand a year, say,
and an automobile and a nice little family in a bungalow
on the edge of town,
that makes the wheels of progress go round!"
- Sinclair Lewis

I wondered what Mother and Faith were doing as we walked down the Dixie Highway. We were looking for a phone, a policeman, anything to get off the dangerous road. Easy wanted us all to hitchhike, but Dad would have none of that.

"You can hitchhike if you want," he told Easy, "but we're calling to get a ride back to your place. Damn cracker," Dad mumbled under his breath, using the derogatory term reserved for ignorant-acting Southern men.

Yikes, I thought, this is getting bad if Dad is resorting to name calling.

The plan for the day hadn't included a blistering hike in the blistering sun.

"Who's going with me this morning?" Dad asked at breakfast one Saturday. "I'll bet we find the right one today."

"Me, me!" I called out.

"I'll go, Dad," Joe answered.

"I'm not going," Mother assured him while feeling my sister's forehead. "I want to keep Faith down today—I don't think she's feeling well." Faith gave a sweetly pathetic look to

185

reinforce the diagnosis. Mother didn't mention the fact that she detested dealing with used car salesmen, whom I only found oddly pushy and very interesting.

"Well, don't expect us before dinner. I want to find a car before The Old Chevy drops dead. That lot over by Johnny-and-Mack's-by-the-Railroad-Tracks had a good ad in the paper." Johnny and Mack's by the Rail Road Tracks was a popular auto body and fender shop that had advertisements all over the city of Miami—radio, television, newspaper.

"If I find a car, I'll come get you so you can drive the Chevy home—or you can drive the new one if you want."

"The Chevy will be fine," Mother assured him, not wanting to spoil the fun of Dad's first day in a new car. "Do you want me to pack a lunch?" Mother asked. That Pennsylvania Dutch frugality thing again.

"No, we'll get a hot dog somewhere," the extravagant Irishman replied.

"Well, get one from a Jewish delicatessen—their meat is good. And let me send some ice water. You know the public drinking fountains aren't kept clean," Mother offered.

Dad quickly finished his two eggs, toast, and coffee, the pronunciation of which Joe and I had pointed out was really, "twegs, toast, and coffee," more accurately representing how our father ordered his standard morning fare, as if Mother and everyone else didn't know it by heart.

Joe and I did not dawdle at breakfast. We enjoyed trips into the seedy world of junk yards and used car lots. Joe was especially anxious to get another car since he'd soon be getting his learner's permit. He had been seen with Mikey—who now went by Mike—with their heads under the hood of The Old Chevy, or taking turns starting it up and driving back and forth in the side yard for hours at a time. The Old Chevy would become Joe's when he needed it for high school activities.

At the boys' request, Mother had taken her worn out chenille bedspread and had made new seat covers to hide the original thread-bear, scratchy wool covers, like camouflaging abrasive weeds with a fuzzy pink bouquet. Dad had removed the running boards to modernize the car. Quite a slick model now, and only 15 years old.

Dad did not leap into many decisions, especially those involving something as costly as a car, and he'd spent many nights and Saturdays scouring the lots and ads for just the right one. He hadn't had a brand new car since Mother's Packard, and that had been traded down during the war as we babies arrived and they needed a four-door vehicle. Having taken the let's-watch-the-odometer-turn-to-100,000-miles ride years ago, we definitely would be moving up from The Old Chevy, yet I knew I was going to miss watching the road speed by through the holes in the floor.

To get to the used car sales area, we drove over toward North Miami and passed the neon church cross which flashed "Jesus Saves" twenty-four hours a day. I liked making up answers to what Jesus saved. Today's guess was Blue Chip stamps. I smiled to myself but wisely did not share this blasphemous gem with Dad. I'd tell Joe later.

Down past the shady banyan trees whose woody shoots grew next to the huge tan trunks, and looked like elephants walking with canes. Past the LeJune Drive-In movie—*Three Coins in a Fountain* was playing—and finally to the car lots.

"I haven't been to Easy Eddie's before," Dad informed Joe and me. "They had the ad in the paper. Let's start here."

We pulled into the lot and parked beneath the billboard caricature of Easy Eddie, and when the original appeared, I realized the caricature was more accurately a fine portrait. Easy Eddie had teeth the size of a horse's and worked his mouth around them in a revolving circle, like a mule eating briars, Joe

187

whispered. His coloring was that of a used-to-be redhead, with large, flat freckles plastered on face and arms. Although his very wavy hair was now graying, his eyebrows were still red, and his eyes were a deep, clear blue.

"Do you think that's Easy Eddie?" I asked Joe, nodding to the billboard. Joe grinned, acknowledging my reference to the accuracy of the portrayal.

"Oh, yeah," he agreed. "That's Easy Eddie all right."

"Why do you think he calls himself easy?" I asked.

"Because he wants you to think it's easy to talk him down on the price."

Dad was out of the car and shaking hands with Easy. Joe and I climbed out, too.

"Ya got a trade in?" Easy inquired.

"No, we'll pay cash," Dad replied. Easy grinned and breathed a sigh of relief, knowing he wouldn't have to unload The Old Chevy on some other victim.

As we walked over to "a nice little vehicle," I studied Easy's clothes. Short-sleeved nearly see-through white nylon summer shirt with yellowing armpits, necktie with the State of Florida sketched on it, along with two cheerleaders throwing a volleyball from the University of Miami to Florida State in Gainesville, which made Joe develop both a sudden interest in Florida geography and his college plans. Plaid Bermuda shorts, black ankle-high socks, and old white and black spectator wingtip shoes.

"He looks like that vaudeville guy on the *Sealtest Big Top*," I reminded Joe.

"Vaudeville guys don't wear Bermudas," he informed me.

Easy and Dad had begun the graceful dance of the used car sale, which was accompanied by a counterpoint harmonic melody composed of Easy's describing every detail of the car in glowing terms, and Dad's responding with critical comments about most of them.

"Here's a beauty," Eddie began. "She's only got 15,000 miles on her."

"Probably rolled back," Dad countered.

"Oh, no we wouldn't take a car that was rolled back," Easy assured us, looking somewhat hurt and like Elmer Gantry at the same time.

"Gets twenty miles to the gallon."

"Around town?"

"New paint job."

"Covering the Bondo here."

"New tires."

Now, this was Dad's forte. The tire kick. "Nice skins," he conceded, after a few swift, well-placed strikes.

Ahh, a weak spot, Easy Eddie detected.

"I could let 'er go for three fifty," Easy suggested.

"Too rich for my blood," Dad replied, although Joe and I knew the budget was five hundred dollars. "Do you have any General Motors cars? I like GM cars."

Easy moved over to a Chevy not much newer than ours.

"No," Dad commanded as he pulled out his crushed pack of Camels and lit one up.

Easy was getting uneasy. He pulled a wad of toothpicks out of his front shirt pocket, chose just the right one, put the others back, and began working the pick around his mouth.

"I do have a newer Chevy out back. Just came in. Only five hundred."

We followed Easy into the garage where a mechanic winked at him. Joe and I both picked up on the wink, and felt obligated to report the signal to Dad in hoarse whispers.

"He winked at Easy Eddie," Joe told Dad out of the side of his mouth.

"What?" Dad asked.

"The mechanic winked at Easy Eddie," I said louder.

"What?" Dad asked again.

"THE MECHANIC WINKED AT EASY EDDIE," I yelled.

This time Dad heard, as did Easy and the mechanic.

"Oh, he's just friendly," Easy assured us. Joe raised his eyebrows and we moved on.

Out back was a 1954 Chevy four door. Easy Eddie and Dad performed a Hokey-Pokey-like verbal dance of the requisite listing of qualities and the requisite retort of faults. Finally, we climbed in for a test drive. Easy Eddie insisted on going with us and riding shotgun in the front seat, which insulted Joe, who was used to the position of honor when Mother wasn't present.

Dad wheeled the car out onto Flagler Street and headed over to the beach, where he could get out of stop-and-go traffic and onto the Dixie Highway.

Once in the close confines of the car, we noted that Easy Eddie had the annoying habit of clearing a post nasal problem with a less-than-pleasant snorting noise. He punctuated most sentences with the snort, and probably was long beyond even knowing he was doing it. Joe and I looked at each other and shuddered.

"Did I tell ya I'm goin' to see Preacher Rollo at the lodge tonight? Snort." Preacher Rollo was the leader of both a small church and a Dixieland band. He'd been on Arthur Godfrey's Talent Scouts when they visited Miami, but he didn't win. Still, he had a large local following, and Easy was obviously proud of his cultural endeavors and wanted Dad to know he was dealing with more than just your average used car salesman.

"We saw Preacher Rollo at Southwest Junior High," I informed Easy, who looked somewhat disappointed that I was honing in on his glory.

190

"Pretty red color, isn't she, kids? Snort."

"Yes," I nodded, but I knew Mother would think it was too show-offy.

"It has the new Chevy Drive automatic shift. Snort."

"I like a stick shift," Dad responded as he made a left onto the Dixie Highway, which then was just a busy wide road.

We drove a few miles at forty-five miles per hour, and as Dad continued to gun the accelerator, the car sputtered, slowed, and stopped.

"Why'd ya stop?" Easy inquired.

"I didn't stop on purpose," Dad responded.

"Maybe we're outa gas," Easy suggested.

"But the gas gauge reads 'full,'" Dad protested.

"Well, I haven't had the car checked out yet. Snort," Easy offered.

Dad and Easy pushed the car back to a filling station we'd seen about a half mile back as Joe steered, and I trotted along, wishing I'd brought the jars of ice water with me instead of letting them melt back at Easy's lot.

Arriving at the Shell station, Dad and I were perspiring, and Easy was nearly terminal, coughing, gasping, and sweating so much that the nylon shirt now stuck to his skin, exposing his wet, hairy chest and back.

"Jesus Christ, it's hot," Easy declared.

"Watch your mouth," Dad growled. "Fill 'er up with ethyl, Mack," he called to the attendant.

"Oh, I don't use ethyl. Snort," Easy managed to sputter out.

"Well, I do," Dad growled again.

"But I don't have any money with me," Easy pleaded.

"Just put a dollar in, Mack," Dad told the attendant, pulling a wrinkled bill out of his wallet. "You can pay me back later, Eddie."

Mack, whose real name was Johnny, put a dollar's worth of ethyl in the car, and Easy announced we needed drinks. Dad, who would have loved a Coke or a Nehi orange, guided us to the water fountain, having spent as much money as he wanted on Easy. As we climbed back into the car for another try, I realized we'd already broken one of Mother's rules—no public drinking fountains.

We continued driving up the Dixie Highway, and Dad fiddled with anything he could reach—the glove compartment, the cigarette lighter, the radio endlessly.

"Pretty good reception, Snort," Easy pointed out.

"I can't find my favorite station," Dad growled.

Their word games were getting tedious.

Dad wanted to take the car up to fifty-five miles per hour and accelerated again. This time we heard a bang and a hiss, and the car stopped again. On checking the rear, Dad and Easy found a flat tire.

"I thought you said this car had good skins," Dad exploded.

"No you said that," Easy snapped. "It does have good tires. Snort. You must have picked up a nail," Easy reprimanded, like Dad had destroyed his valuable vehicle.

"Well, roll your sleeves up, Eddie," Dad commanded. "You have a tire to change."

A look of incredulity passed over Easy's uneasy face.

"Well, sure, I'll help," he answered. Double snort.

"The hell you say," Dad blasted. "I'll hand you the tools."

No Shakespeare quotations today, I thought, noting that I'd have to report Dad's swearing to Mother.

Dad needn't have bothered about who handed whom the tools. There were no tools. There was no spare tire. After all, Easy hadn't had a chance to have the car checked out.

192

"Okay!" Dad commanded, "You're pushing this baby back to the filling station."

"But that's two or three miles," Easy Eddie complained. Snort.

"Okay," Dad softened, "We'll all walk back and call your mechanic to come get us."

By this time it was about eleven, and the sun was almost directly overhead.

"Let's hitchhike," Easy suggested again.

"You can hitchhike if you want," Dad told him, "but we're calling to get a ride back to your place."

Joe and I alternated between running and letting Dad catch up. Easy Eddie lagged behind, suffering more than any of us in the sun. Car after car whizzed by, but none stopped for his extended thumb.

A nice older couple going the opposite direction did stop on the other side of the road to see if we were all right, and Dad asked if they'd flag down a policeman if they saw one. Apparently they didn't see any police because around noon we dragged back into the Shell station. Dad got his first good look at Easy Eddie for the first time since we abandoned the car, and was alarmed at his condition. He gave Eddie a nickel and told him to call his mechanic to come and get us. As we waited in the relative coolness of the filling station office, we noticed a machine with some hot dogs of questionable age, turning over and over on the long spikes.

"What the hell," Dad shrugged, as if he'd finally given up trying to make a go of the day. "We'll take four hot dogs, Mack."

Mack handed us each a greenish-tan frankfurter on a stale bun and offered a jar of mustard.

"How 'bout drinks, folks?" he offered.

Easy Eddie was getting excited. "I'd like a Coke," he

answered.

"No, just four hot dogs," Dad countered—their dance was continuing. "We'll just use the water fountain."

Easy was dejected, and so was I. The cold, sharp taste of a Coke sounded good. Easy bolted his hot dog down in about thirty seconds and began throwing broad hints, which only a person in a coma wouldn't pick up on, about another hot dog. Dad just ignored him. About a half-hour later, the winking mechanic appeared in one of their "nice little vehicles," and we climbed in for the silent drive back to the car lot.

As we got out of the car, Easy Eddie, always the professional, actually told Dad, "Well, make me an offer. Snort."

"An offer on what?" Dad asked, thinking of several things he could offer Easy Eddie.

"On the little Chevy out on the highway."

Joe looked at me. I looked at Dad. Dad looked at both of us, and we began a giggling noise like shy hyenas. Finally, Dad regained his composure, requesting the $1.60 he'd spent on gasoline and hot dogs, and assured Easy Eddie we would not be interested in a car that day, but thanks for asking.

We climbed back into The Old Chevy, which by then seemed pretty good to us, and drove off. I looked back and saw Easy Eddie picking his teeth while looking both hurt and like Elmer Gantry again.

"Bye, folks. Snort," I heard him call out above the roar of our car.

"Well, you're home early," Mother observed as we came through the front door. "Any luck?"

Having agreed to eliminate any disturbing stories about our day, we reported on having seen some real beauties of cars, having eaten some delicious Jewish deli wieners, as well as having finished her thoughtful water bottles. I guess if you have your fingers crossed behind your back, lies of mercy don't matter so much.

"I think we'll get a new car, Isabel. No more used ones," Dad told Mother. "I just think it's time for a brand new car."

Having heard the news, Joe and I decided the day had been worth the hassle, if we didn't get food poisoning. We got into our bathing suits and jumped in the deliciously cool pool, and began our Easy Eddie imitations.

Snort.

Snort. Snort.

Chapter 33

"Whom they have injured they also hate."
- Seneca

Even with the odd Pennsylvania Dutch speech pattern, our heritage idiosyncracies really didn't bother us much. Lots of other children had ethnic roots. We met many people whose cultures were also sometimes noticeable—Jewish people, Polish people, Cuban people, Puerto Rican people, but few black people, just Otis-the-Egg-Man and the Cunningham's maid.

Florida was thoroughly segregated in those days, and xenophobia ran rampant. Segregation actually serves an important purpose—it provides poor, white, uneducated individuals someone to feel superior to, at least in their own minds.

We children noticed the separate water fountains and restrooms everyone knows about today. Every time we rode the city bus when we were little, we'd run to the back and hop on the wide leather seat. And every time we did, Mother would whisper the rule and scoot us back up to the smaller seats.

When we were little, we knew there was "colored town" over near the Dixie Highway, where the blacks were forced to live in high-rent shacks. Wealthier minority citizens were permitted to support the local merchants by spending money on nice clothes and automobiles. We knew there was a small back waiting room and entrance at our doctor's office, designed so the ill black patients did not disturb the ill white patients. Driving back home hot and sandy and sunburned from Crandon Park, the fully developed county beach, we saw dark people on Virginia Beach, the primitive beach reserved for skin darker than Cuban. We saw these differences and as little children did not question them.

Having grown up in an integrated state and having been educated, my parents did their best to teach respect and acceptance of all races and religions. Those third grade months in an integrated northern school introduced the reality of my parents' theory to me.

On my return to Florida, I had told Joe about my black schoolmates. He nodded in understanding, and we got down to the business of serious outdoor play. The subject was tabled, but as national awareness increased and some of the information actually trickled down into Southern journalism, it resurfaced.

Among the neighborhood kids, we found ourselves the only ones interested in talking about integration. Laurie Ann and her brother said they didn't care one way or the other. They were from Illinois and were bored by the subject, and let's get out the bat and play Indian ball. Joe's friend Mikey thought the Negroes were strong workers and good singers, but also thought it was funny we'd take their side. Litlle-Alabama-Born-Linda-Down-the-Street was angry with me for "goin' against God's will."

We learned integration wasn't a good topic for neighborhood discussion. So when Ralph Reneck reported the local news and Douglas Edwards reported the national news on WTVJ Channel 4, we'd watch the trouble in the Deep South with our parents, but we'd say nothing outside the house. Until eighth grade.

My family spent several weeks the summer between

my seventh and eighth grades in the Blue Mountains outside Kingston, Jamaica. It was there we were introduced to blacks who were treated with much more respect than they were in Miami, although most still seemed to be limited to the service occupations. The Blue Mountains were somewhat isolated from the cities of Kingston and Montego Bay, and the racial barriers were less noticeable.

I won't lie and say I was not without my own share of xenophobia, but I think it was more for a man than for a black man. Left in the rental car on a back road in Kingston while our parents went into the local agency to apply for tourist drivers' licenses, Faith and I were duly frightened when a native began bothering us through the windows of the car. We'd tried to get the doors locked without insulting the man, a sort of subtle shift-in-the-seat-and-hit-the-lock-with-the-elbow routine, but he would not go away. I'd heard about girls and women being attacked by men, and felt my moment may be imminent.

Without mentioning the sex part, I voiced my fears to Joe in my best ventriloquist performance—thank heaven for the weekly training we received watching *Paul Winchell and Jerry Mahoney* on TV. Lips motionless and teeth slightly apart, it went something like, "Hoe, I think he lay de dangerous."

Joe quietly turned around in the seat and told me, "Just ignore him. Dad and Mom will be out in a minute, and I'll take care of things if I have to. And don't be a dope, Mercy, with the ventriloquism."

Sitting back, I decided to make my totally unvoluptuous self less appealing, just in case. Wearing my hair in a ponytail without bangs that day, appearing more skinned rat than Marilyn Monroe, I needn't have bothered, but just the same I went to work uglying up. I threw my fully mobile ears back and out, sucked my small chin into oblivion, made my teeth buck out, and squinted. Soon my parents reappeared. Seeing me through the window, Mother was startled and asked if I was sick. My father gave the man some change, got in the car, and drove away.

When we weren't off sightseeing in the rental car or swimming in the pool, Faith Rose played with the child of a maid from the lodge, and Joe and I tagged along after the chauffer—a patient gentleman—helping him shine the station wagon and learning a few things about the island. During our time in downtown Kingston, we were exposed to blacks who spoke the Queen's English, to policemen dressed in immaculate white uniforms, to women with baskets balanced atop their stately bodies, and to the wonderful sounds of the island musicians. Our Jamaica experience not only reinforced our parents' philosophy of acceptance, it took it to the next step—appreciation.

When school started in the fall, the Phys Ed teachers held a girls' softball tournament to celebrate the World Series. I was elected captain of our homeroom team, and the games began. We had enthusiasm, but only one of us was any good at softball. Sonja was new in school, having recently moved up from Puerto Rico, and was such a strong hitter that we placed her fourth on the batting order. Assuming some of the previous three hitters could at least get to first base by toppling the ball somewhere between home plate and the pitcher's box, we felt Sonja could bring them home. One person cannot save a team, but between Sonja's athleticism and the other teams' forfeiting games by not showing up, we managed to win the tournament, and having survived combat, we girls had become close allies.

Consequently, when Sonja was absent from school for several days in a row, we began asking what was wrong. Was she sick? Appendicitis? A broken limb? After many inquiries,

Mr. Lincoln, our home room teacher, reluctantly told us in confidence that Sonja had been sent to the "colored school" over in Coconut Grove. She was too dark for ours.

Thus, when Mrs. Mitchell, our dynamic speech teacher, assigned pairs to prepare debates, I took the affirmative position on abolishing school segregation. Susan, my best friend at school and a strict Southern Baptist, took the opposing view. Since we did not have to report our topics to our teacher, we simply began forming arguments, composed mainly and most unscholarly of our own opinions.

When it was time for our presentation, Susan and I pulled chairs up to the large table, shuffled papers, and announced our topic. Mrs. Mitchell must have been busy in the back of the room because she didn't stop us immediately. I postulated, "All schools should be integrated." But before I could continue, Mrs. Mitchell jumped up and called out for us to stop, immediately. She said it was against Florida State law to discuss segregation in the public schools. Amazed and dazed, I walked back to my desk. It was my epiphany: No matter what my parents and others felt was Right, something very, very Wrong was going on. We could not discuss a controversial topic, especially *that* controversial topic. What better way to protect and perpetuate a concept than to make it illegal to discuss at school. No new ideas for new citizens.

After class, Mrs. Mitchell tried to rectify the situation, "Mercy, I'm sorry I had to cancel your debate—I'd be happy to give you another chance for your grade." But I could regurgitate no situation-smoothing lie, and left the classroom.

That night, my father told me that, apparently, we did not have freedom of speech in school in Florida, but when I suggested that very issue be my new topic, he advised me to drop the subject—the time was not right. We'd had the same conversation when my history teacher said that slavery played only an insignificant role in the Civil War.

Susan and I received our usual A's when we argued the pros and cons of going steady.

Chapter 34

"I cannot tell how the truth may be;
I say the tales as 'twas told to me."
- Sir Walter Scott

I'd learned as much about the Graces as I could handle or wanted to handle, and the stories were tucked away in my memory, ready to be resurrected when I needed them. There was now little time spent pondering the past. A new, urgent element of socialization was in my life.

I thought my quest for Uncle John information was over, but once the gate of his whereabouts was opened, more and more details started flowing in.

Dear Helen,

How are you? I am fine. Well, I finally found out. But I was not supposed to tell anyone, but it has been 4 years and I HAVE TO TELL SOMEONE or I'll burst!

Uncle John is not a Nazi war criminal like we thought, even though his name is German. No wonder the lady at the library thought we were being mean when we asked her if she had any information about Nazis living in Ohio.

When we were visiting Aunt Edna last year, Joe and my mom and dad went to visit him. That was the day Faith and I stayed at your house and Betsy found your dad's empty beer bottles and drank all the drops and fell asleep on the footstool and your mom got so mad at your dad. Well that was the day. Do you like my new writing? I am trying to be more careful with it. Well, Joe said they drove about two hours and got to this big old place that looks like the Biltmore Hotel here but not so fancy and getting pretty old and they have a big wall and gate and a man to let them go in. They went to an office. Then Joe and Dad waited on the lawn and Mom visited Uncle John. Mom could not find out where all the things were that she sent him in his room and she thinks they just take what they want and don't give it to Uncle John. A really weird man came by. He called Joe a bumble bee over and over and he said he was sort of scared and sort of mad and the man was really weird, but Dad said just be friendly and keep on reading your book. Then Mom and Uncle John came out and he remembered Joe and hugged him and shook hands with my dad. They ate the picnic my mom packed and then Mom took Uncle John back inside. Then my mom cried and they left and Joe saw the sign Ohio Hospital for Mental so Uncle John is crazy. I guess I should feel bad but I don't really know him. I just wanted to know where he was and now I know and I do not like knowing. Mom finally said yes Uncle John is a mental patient and he has to have electric treatments and even had an operation on his brain and probably will live in the hospital for mental forever. She cries whenever she talks about him, so I don't talk about him to her anymore.

Dad says we watch too much TV and he got really mad when we stayed at a house behind us watching TV for so long that he had to drive all over looking for us and when he found us he said we would get a spanking. Joe said he was too old for a spanking and Dad said ok you have to polish my shoes and gave us each one and when we were done he said they looked good but we did a lousy job and he gave us a quarter anyway and told him not to watch TV so much and don't scare our parents out of their wits. So now I have $3.86 and I am going to buy Faith a color book and me a Archie comic and Joe some glue for his models and save the rest for a rainy day like Dad says but why should we save for a rainy day? Don't tell anyone about Uncle John. Mom said we couldn't. But I tell you everything.

Love, Mercy

P.S. Tell Bobby hey and I am still his girlfriend.

And so Uncle John continued living at the Ohio State Mental Hospital, enduring the barbaric practices mental patients received for another ten or fifteen years, until the psychotropic medications changed the face of psychiatric treatment.

Even as a young child, I knew something was terribly wrong when Uncle John went missing, but I had no idea it was bad enough that the family felt it necessary to lie, evade, and generally cover up what was considered in those days a disgrace.

Looking back, I think my Nazi theory was a convenient way to dismiss the subtle clues I overheard, letters I snooped into, and discrepancies in family stories. Searching for a Nazi war criminal was much easier to endure than mourning the tragic outcome for a beloved relative.

Chapter 35

"Fear not the future,
Weep not for the past."
- Percy Shelly

As we became more and more a part of the church family and made friendships, my best friend there was Angela Perez. She was a Gables kid, a choir member, a school friend, and both of our fathers worked for Pan American Airlines at the time—hers as a pilot and mine as an engineer. Angela's parents had also converted to the Episcopal Church, and because of our daily proximity, we practiced our pre-confirmation catechism together at school. Memorizing the catechism was a lengthy task and required innumerable recitations and corrections until we had it down perfectly.

Angela's wealthy family had left Cuba a few years earlier and was still in the process of helping an uncle, a Havana physician, emigrate up to Miami. Early in the political unrest in Cuba of the 1950s, the Cuban intelligencia had recognized the possible result of the turmoil in their homeland. Many had given up much in order to emigrate, and most of the immigrants were in South Florida. Angela's uncle, Ramon Perez, was planning on working as a waiter in Miami Beach until he could take the Florida State medical boards.

I was charmed by Angela's family. They were warm and dynamic, and with coal black hair and dark, dark eyes, were physically attractive as well. Sometimes they would slip into the rapid, firecracker-like Cuban speech pattern, and because of my rudimentary Spanish lessons in fifth grade, I could occasionally pick out a word or two. It sounded like "clickety-clackety, clickety-clackety, alcolba." Ha. I know that—it's "bedroom." "Clickety-clackety, clickety-clackety, gato." Cat!

Their expensive Spanish-style home was decorated in the ultimate Florida style with real art from the islands and many possessions of Spanish heritage. At our church confirmation, Angela wore her mother's lace wedding mantilla while the rest of us girls wore the church-supplied veils, which looked like small sheer tablecloths. The Perez family was a joy to watch.

Cuba had been involved in organized crime for many years, and President Batista was gaining treasure at the expense of the Cuban people. Then in 1952, Fidel Castro, a Havana attorney, led an uprising in Havana which was quickly crushed by the Cuban military establishment. The next year President Batista granted asylum to political prisoners, and Castro chose exile in the United States and Mexico rather than spending any more time in jail. But it was not over. In 1956, Castro and Che Guevara, a medical doctor, once again attempted to overtake the increasingly unpopular Batista government, and the uprising was again crushed. The two fled to the mountains with their followers, where they carried out guerilla tactics and gained yet more support. When crime and capitalism flourish at the expense of the populace, communism easily slips in.

We felt the effects of Cuba's unrest in Miami in the early days, way before the Bay of Pigs and the Mariel Boat Lift. Father Carroll, as the newspaper headline read, had blasted the political turmoil from the pulpit. There was talk of war so close to our state, and there was talk of economic upset—the sugar cane, the rum, the cigars. Even Joe's Air Scout troop had to buy different uniforms before the boys flew to Havana for a week-long tour of the island. Their sky blue twills looked too much like Batista's Secret Police uniforms, and the folks at Pan

American, the troop's sponsor, felt the boys could be put in jeopardy if mistaken for Batista's squad.

Then it was 1959. Castro finally had gained power, and only the very young and the very old Cubans were allowed to leave. Being a person of authority, Angela's uncle was categorized as dangerous and disappeared, and a stunned gravity enveloped the family. They spent much time praying for him and for the safety of the others trapped in the motherland.

In addition to the political trauma, we felt other, more subtle changes. No more late-night radio advertisements for the Hotel Nacional de Cuba. The hotel was Castro's new headquarters. No more advertisements for its Dancing Waters act. Chickens and goats roamed the massive marble lobby. No more tourists from Cuba enjoying the shopping and entertainment in Miami. No more pleasure trips to Havana. Less sparkle. Less life. Only a few military at Gitmo—Guantanamo Bay. No more Cuba as we'd known it. Never again.

Although I'd followed the Korean War when I was younger and had routinely checked behind the bathroom door for a hiding North Korean, I'd really never been associated with the horrors of a contemporary war. True, I'd seen women and men around Miami who had identification numbers tattooed on their wrists by the Nazis, but, horrifying as the tattoos were, it was ancient history to me—World War II had been over for ten plus years.

I realized the difference between Angela's father and uncle was just a matter of timing—when each actually tried to leave Cuba. The juxtaposition of Angela's and my secure lives in Miami against her uncle's immediate jeopardy became a vivid dichotomy one afternoon as we sat on her mahogany bed and recited catechism:

"I believe in one God, the Father Almighty, maker of heaven and earth, and all things visible and invisible . . .

Banging on the front door of the expensive Ramon Perez home in suburban Havana . . .

"And in one Lord Jesus Christ, the only begotten Son of God . . .

"Ramon Perez, open this door. Ramon Perez, open the door. You cannot hide."

"Begotten, not made. Being of one substance with the father, by whom all things were made . . .

Ramon's wife and children flee to the back of the house, and Ramon unchains the lock on the front door.

"Who for us men and for our salvation came down from heaven, and was made incarnate by the Holy Ghost of the Virgin Mary, and was made man . . .

Castro's army seizes Ramon Perez, handcuffs him, and leads him to the truck.

"And was crucified for us under Pontius Pilate. He suffered and was buried . . .

The prison is dark and damp, and the men take turns scaring away the rats at night.

"And the third day he rose again according to the Scriptures, and ascended into heaven, and is seated on the right hand of the Father . . .

"Ramon Perez, come with me, you must see El General "

"And he will come again in glory to judge both the quick and the dead, and his kingdom will have no end . . .

"Ramon Perez, you are convicted of being a political enemy of the people."

"And I believe in the Holy Ghost, the Lord and Giver of Life. . .Who with the Father and the Son is worshipped and glorified. Who spake by the Prophets . . .

"Take him away. He will remain in prison the remainder of his life."

"And I believe in one Catholic and Apostolic Church.

I acknowledge one Baptism for the remission of sins . . .

"Do not worry, Señor, we need a doctor in my village. I will see that you escape."

"And I look for the Resurrection of the dead, and the Life of the world to come. Amen."

Chapter 36

"...a friend is someone who knows us, but loves us anyway."
- Fr. Jerome Cummings

As the years rolled by, we had lost touch with the Jameses, as so often happens with former neighbors. We were stunned when we read Bertha's obituary in the *Miami Gazette*— They described her as the most loyal reader and writer of their small weekly paper. Mother and I immediately drove over to the James' house and spent the afternoon with Roy. We began cleaning the kitchen while Roy sat at the table, telling us the awful story of Bertha's death.

"You know Bertha was active in public service," Roy began matter-of-factly. He was referring to her letters to the editors, "and she was the best cane caller around. I think she shoulda been proud how she went, even though it was awful."

Yes, I thought, I remember the first time Bertha ran to the front porch of our rental house and yelled, "Cane's a comin!" In addition to being the local *Gazette* volunteer correspondent, Bertha was the neighborhood meteorological Paul Revere, running to every house on the block. She would have gone to every middlesex, village, and farm, I thought, if there were any nearby.

Bertha felt a hurricane in her right big toe substantially before the weatherman came on WTVJ to report one was on the way.

"Ever since I was a girl," Bertha had explained to

Mother and me soon after we moved in, "I'd wake up and be real sore in my toe, and the next thing you knew, a cane was a comin'." She pointed to the big one on her right foot, and the size and crookedness indeed made it look as if it could be used for more than just walking. It was large, fleshy, and sported a huge bunion-like growth on the knuckle. With thick, dry skin and cracked nail, it was a toe you didn't want to touch, even if you were paid to like the salesmen at the nice shoe stores in the Gables or a doctor or a nurse. I had eliminated those career possibilities based on the mental image I carried of Bertha's big toe.

The Jameses and most of the neighbors believed in the toe connection to hurricanes, but Bertha did confess to Mother about the unfortunate morning when her toe was sore and she ran around two blocks yelling, "Cane's a comin'!" only to find out later the sore toe was due to the shoes she'd bought at "Woolsworth," as she called the nice five and dime in downtown Miami. "They was a half size too small, but they was cheap," she explained later that day, "But, hey, even that meteor guy on TV gets it wrong sometimes," she added with no apology to Mr. Conklin who was called home from work unnecessarily when his wife Wanda telephoned to report the status of Bertha's toe. Wanda and Bertha didn't get along too well after that.

When Bertha knew a cane was a comin', she would locate Roy, who was generally not far from the house, and start directing the hurricane preparations—nailing boards over the windows of the little rental house, filling jars with water, rounding up their hen Miss Lucy and rooster Bucky Boy, scooting them into the shed, and, of course, sprinkling Tide on all the floors. When everything around the house was ready, Bertha and Roy would grab a couple of blankets and head to the shelter at the elementary school.

I jerked myself back to the present and paid attention to

214

Roy's story.

"You know," he continued, "we thought a cane was a comin' last Tuesday 'cause Bertha woke up with this awful pain in her toe. Nothing would do but she get right out of bed before daybreak and start callin' up and down the street. I seen lights flip on all down the block, and I started gettin' Miss Emily and Binky Boy rounded up. You know Miss Lucy and Bucky Boy died about four years ago, and now we have Miss Emily and Binky Boy. That Bertha loved her chickens, she did. Do you want to take some eggs home? We have extras all over in that box in the corner." Mother declined, saying she had just bought several dozen, which I knew was a lie.

"Bertha came back and reminded me to sprinkle the Tide on the floors and nail up the windows. She was always so particular about things, bless her little heart. That's why we lived so good." Roy choked up and had to stop talking for a minute or two. Then he began again, "We done got to the school just as the principal was a gettin' there, and he told Bertha he couldn't set up a shelter until the superintendent called.

"Bertha and me just hung around and jawed with the janitor for a while, waitin' for the call. She had some real good ideas for the janitor on cutting down on his work load, like havin' the teachers empty their own dern trash cans ever afternoon. Well, anyway, even though Bertha's toe jus got worse and worse, no call came. The principal done called the TV station and they said the meteor guy had no cane a comin'. Bertha just couldn't understand it—this was the worst her toe ever done hurt. I asked her if she'd been a wearin' them tight shoes again, and she said no she hadn't. I think I hurt her feelins that I was soundin' like I was doubtin' her.

"Finally, I says honey bunch lets us jus' go home and wait. It'll come and they'll be openin' the shelter soon. This seemed to satisfy Bertha, and besides she needed to be gettin' that toe up or soakin' or somethin', it was a hurtin' so bad."

"Roy, had Bertha ever gone to a doctor about her toe?" Mother asked innocently enough.

Roy snapped his head up and looked as if he'd been wounded by her question. "Why should we spend good money on them dern doctors? They cause more harm than good. Bertha hadn't been to a doctor in her whole life." Mother refrained from asking any more questions.

"Well, anyway, she soaked that toe and put it up on the coffee table, but nothin' helped. By that time we had Wanda down the street a bangin' on our door demandin' where the cane was. I told her it was a comin' late this time. Then Wanda just bargted in and told Bertha thank you very much for making her mister late to work and his boss didn't believe in Bertha's toe.

"Poor Bertha. She just got white and couldn't talk or nothin'. Wanda and me got real worried and Wanda said she was a callin' a amblance even though I told her we didn't' believe in them doctors or hospitals neither. Well the amblance showed up with its light a whirlin' and screamin' and took her over to Jackson Memorial, but by the time we got there she was gone. Poor little thing just went to sleep in the amblance.

"I just can't believe it was such an awful death for Bertha. Havin' to go in an amblance on the way to a hospital after no one believed her about the toe. It was a terrible death," Roy kept repeating.

"Did the doctor ever say what she died of, Roy?" Mother dared to ask.

"He said it was a heart attack, but he done never seen no one have the pain in a toe before, but I tole him that wasn't just any toe, it was a special toe." Mother and I nodded our heads in agreement.

"Well, Roy, we're just so sorry," Mother began. "There's

not much we can do for her now except help take good care of you." She began writing a list on the back of the electric bill envelope. "We'll come over once a week and keep things up for you."

There you go, Mother, I thought, everything is fixed by cleaning and organizing.

"Don't you bother that, Isabel," Roy told Mother. "I done always kept this place up real good 'cause Bertha was so busy with her newspaper work. I know how to keep a house real good."

As we climbed in the car, Roy told me, "Honey, tell yer daddy that Bertha gave her life to public service. Even if that cane never did come, she was a tryin'. And what will the paper do without her? They won't have nothin' good to read no more."

I started to pull my little leather notebook out of my purse—I thought this an important enough occasion to use it for the first time. I'd been saving it for good. But, instead, I reached over, picked up the envelope from the electricity bill, and added a few key words to the list so that I'd be able to report Roy's message to Dad.

I did not have to spoil my pretty leather notebook. I'd become my mother.

Chapter 37

"When shall we . . .meet again,
In thunder, lightening, or in rain?
When the hurlyburly's done,
When the battle's lost and won."
- William Shakespeare

Our days in Florida were coming to an end. They were our salad days—the carefree days of early flourishing. Our Miami days were the days of a year-round summer and of running around half naked in our bathing suits and then jumping in the pool to cool off and then starting to run around again.

The days of the Kool-Aid wagon, delivering door-to-door sticky drinks up and down the block, and reading, and Miss Lily and overhalls. Bob Rose's mistaking everyone. Bertha and Roy and Blow Outs and a hurricane toe. Easy Eddie's used cars. Tom Thumbs. Joe's clubhouse, Cuba, and eating grass.

They were the days we lost Baby Sugar and our grandmother, and found new friends and wondered about Uncle John and learned the truth, and gained a sadness we didn't really understand.

The days we grew and matured and began to branch out to find our own selves. Snuggling next to Mother and eating huge bowls of potato chips while watching *Perry Mason* on TV. Dances and dippy ekks and the Rexall twins. Rigid Pennsylvania Dutchmen in a relaxed, flamboyant town.

In Miami, we kids expected the world to treat us well, and it usually did. There was no life-altering trauma like the

Great Depression to define our generation. At least not until 1963. We lived our lives under a parasol of optimism, rather than under an umbrella of deprivation. It was the time of our Miami paradise, and I didn't think we'd ever again be the same. I told Mother we'd get back to the South some day, and the sun would still be there, waiting for both of us.

I know the time for a move seemed right—Mother was ready for another adventure, and Dad was ready for a change of career scenery. When the offer from Boeing arrived, we prepared the house for selling and prepared ourselves for the long trip. At the time, we had no idea where we were going or what we were getting into, and it sounded like a grand journey.

Our friends at church gave Joe and me a nice party the night before we left. They had a cake, and Father Carroll handed each of us a St. Christopher's medal for safe traveling. He puffed his cheeks at me, for old time's sake, I guess. Then the group sang the going-away song:

"We're so·rry you're go·ing a·way, we wi·ish that yo·ou could stay. Oh, how we'll miss you, we wish we could kiss you. We're so·rry you're go·ing a·way."

A few girls hugged me and a few boys shook Joe's hand. Then we strolled the night away in the new line dance.

"Let's go stroh·oh·ling" was still playing in my head the next morning as I went from room to room, telling my house goodbye.

"Goodbye, bedroom. Goodbye plaster outlines on the wall and little closet and current Roach Hotel."

"Goodbye, Joe's room and workbench and cowboys and Indians." I sure hope Joe gets something more grown up in Seattle.

"Goodbye, bathroom." Still no North Korean hiding

220

behind the door.

"Goodbye hallway." I still can hear the wind from the hurricanes.

"Goodbye Florida room and lounge chairs." Dad loved enjoying the breeze with you every evening.

"Goodbye pool." Oh, goodbye pool. You were the best part. You were my favorite part. Goodbye everything."

Goodbye mercies and goodbye graces.

Joe stood behind me and scratched his head in bewilderment. What will she do next? His practical mind must have wondered.

Anxious to begin our new journey and our new life, we shouted and ran to the loaded-down station wagon, and climbed into the back seat with our little Faith Rose between us, and drove off.

Our Florida days were our days of smiles and good neighbors and friends, and US, and then they were gone forever.

No one can tell, but I've kept that Florida feeling in a special part of my heart. It's always there, and I bring it out when I need some sunshine for my soul.

BOOK CLUB DISCUSSION QUESTIONS

[1]   The novel *Lies of Mercy - Lies of Grace* does not follow the traditional pattern for works of fiction (characters put into conflict with complications leading to a climax and conclusion), but rather follows the picaresque pattern (stand-alone chapters that advance the story). Situation comedies and dramas on television follow this pattern. Do you think the picaresque pattern works for this novel?
Why?

[2]   Does the character Mercy "ring true"? Can you identify with her? If not, which character do you have more in common with and why?

[3]   What part does Mercy's Amish and Pennsylvania Dutch heritage play in the family dynamics? Were you able to follow along with the Pennsylvania Dutch expressions? Did they lend to the story? What part does Mercy's Irish heritage play? Describe how you have had some "zig-zags" in your life.

[4]   Describe Mercy's relationship with her siblings. How does being the middle child seem to affect Mercy? Is this consistent with what many people believe about middle children? What exceptions do you find to this viewpoint?

[5]   Which room in the house where you grew up was the most significant in your life? Did another room play a great role also? Why were these rooms so important? What happened in them to affect your decision? Which room seems to be most important to Mercy?

[6]   Why do you think Mercy is so focused on Uncle John? Is it better to tell a child the truth or to keep family secrets? Why were Mercy's relatives so secretive about Uncle John? Is that same dynamic present in today's society, or have the barriers fallen somewhat?

[7]   Why did Mercy sometimes feel out of place in relaxed, flamboyant Miami? Have you ever felt this way in a town or a group? Why?

[8]   Which is your favorite chapter in Lies of Mercy – Lies of Grace? Why? There is a saying, "Do some folks feel happier because you passed their way?" Do you feel happier having read this book? (I certainly hope so! cjp)

Breinigsville, PA USA
25 October 2010
247969BV00001B/3/P

9 780984 243655